Tell Me About
Science &
Technology

Tell Me About
Science &
Technology

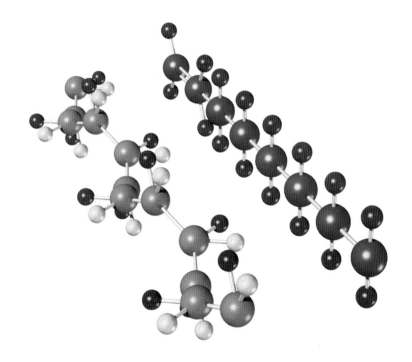

WATERBIRD BOOKS

Columbus, Ohio

School Specialty
Children's Publishing

This edition published in the United States of America in 2004 by
Waterbird Books,
an imprint of School Specialty Children's Publishing,
a member of the School Specialty Family.
8720 Orion Place
Columbus, OH 43240-2111

Printed in China

ISBN 0-7696-3382-X

2 3 4 5 6 7 8 9 10 TOP 10 09 08 07 06 05

CONTENTS

THE
EARTH

CONTENTS

. . . .

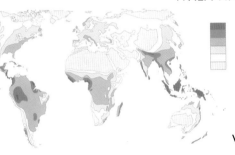

WHEN IS SUMMER SOLSTICE?

The earth revolves around the sun, and at the same time, it revolves on its own axis. As it moves around the sun, it also spins like a top. If the axis of the earth were at right angles to the path of the earth around the sun, all the days of the year would be the same length. However, the earth is tilted at an angle of 66.5°. In June, the northern hemisphere is tilted towards the sun, and it receives more sunshine during the day. This is its warmest season, called *summer*. On June 21, the sun is directly over the Tropic of Cancer. It is midsummer in the northern hemisphere. This is the time known as the summer solstice.

FACT FILE

The sun is the source of light and heat for the solar system. The four planets closest to the sun are small and solid, the closest being Mercury. An asteroid belt separates these from the four larger planets, which are made up of gas.

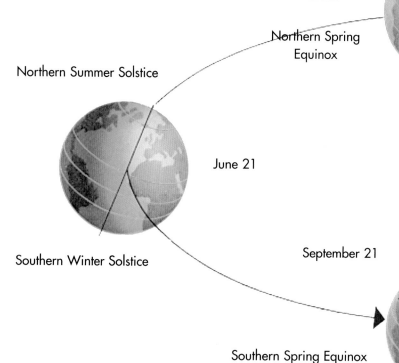

Northern Spring Equinox

Northern Summer Solstice

June 21

Southern Winter Solstice

September 21

Southern Spring Equinox

WHEN IS THE SHORTEST DAY?

FACT FILE

Mars is known as the "Red Planet" because it is covered by a stone desert containing iron oxide, making it appear red. The water and oxygen that used to exist on Mars are now locked up in these iron deposits. So, the planet has hardly any atmosphere.

The shortest day of the year is December 21. It is in the winter solstice. When the northern hemisphere is turned toward the sun, the countries north of the equator have their summer season. The countries south of the equator have their winter season. When the direct rays of the sun fall on the southern hemisphere, it is their summer, and it is winter in the northern hemisphere. There are two days in the year when night and day are equal lengths all over the world. They occur in the spring and fall, halfway between the two solstices. One is the autumnal equinox in September, and the other is the spring equinox in March.

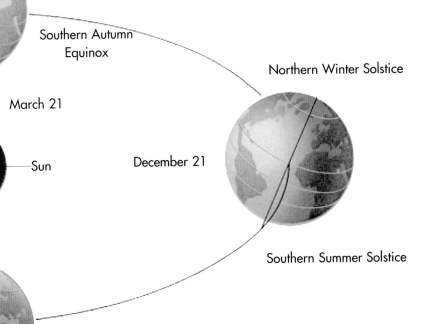

Southern Autumn Equinox

March 21

Sun

December 21

Northern Winter Solstice

Southern Summer Solstice

Northern Spring Equinox

WHY DO OCEANS FREEZE?

In Antarctica and the Arctic, the oceans freeze because the temperatures are so low. Seawater, unlike fresh water, continues to increase in density as its temperature decreases towards the freezing point (about 32°F). In fact, Antarctica contains 90 percent of all the ice on earth. Scientists have calculated that if all this ice melts, sea levels would rise by almost 200 feet, causing world-wide flooding. An accumulation of sea ice can cause an iceberg, which floats in the sea because it is less dense than water.

FACT FILE

Over 220 million square miles of the earth's surface is covered by oceans and seas, with the Pacific Ocean accounting for nearly 36 percent of the total.

An iceberg in a frozen ocean

WHY DO WAVES BREAK?

FACT FILE

For centuries, sailors have been afraid of being sucked into a whirlpool that would swallow their ships. Whirlpools occur when opposing currents meet.

Force or energy is needed to start a wave, and it is the wind that provides this energy in the water. Wind blows the surface layers of the sea, gradually forming a rolling movement of waves. As these waves near the coast, the seabed interrupts their rolling movement. They mount up and break onto the beach.

The water inside a wave moves around and around in a circle. Near the shore, the circular shape of the wave is changed, and it becomes squashed. The top of the wave becomes unstable, so when it hits the beach, it topples and spills over. On beaches with a shallow slope, the waves pile up to a great height before breaking, causing surf.

Angel Falls, Venezuela

HOW DOES WATER WEAR AWAY SOLID ROCK?

FACT FILE

When water seeps through the ground and reaches hot rock or volcanic gases, it boils violently. This produces steam that can shoot the water out of cracks, causing a geyser.

Water itself cannot wear away rock, but tiny particles of sand and dirt carried in the water can eventually wear away even the hardest rocks. It is this continuous wearing process that cuts valleys through mountains and hills. The faster the water flows, the more particles it carries and the more it wears away at the rock. The same process can be seen along the coast. These rocks are worn away by the constant action of sand being thrown against them by the waves.

WHEN DO RIVERS RUN BACKWARD?

In the former Soviet Union, the direction of several rivers was diverted or reversed to provide water for irrigation. Some of the rivers running into the Aral Sea were diverted northward in a huge water management project designated to irrigate land north of the region. In some cases, the direction of their flow was reversed. The result was that the Aral Sea began to dry up because no more river water flowed into it.

Reversed flowing water

Sometimes, the flow is reversed naturally, but this only happens in very large rivers when very high tides overcome the normal river currents. In narrow parts of the river valley, the water begins to pile up, and eventually, a wave called a *tidal bore* passes back up the river, sometimes for a great distance.

FACT FILE

Tidal bores happen in the Amazon in South America, where bores can be as high as 14.75 feet. A smaller bore travels up the River Severn in England.

WHY DO EARTHQUAKES OCCUR?

Our planet is a very restless place. Every 30 seconds, the ground rumbles and trembles. Most of the movements are so slight that they are not felt. Others can be so large that they cause complete disaster. Big cracks appear in the land, streets buckle, and buildings crumble. In fact, whole towns and cities can be destroyed. This occurence is called an *earthquake*. It is caused by the moving of the earth's crust, called *plates*. When these plates slide past or into each other, the rocks jolt and send out shock waves.

FACT FILE

Mining operations are known to have caused earthquakes in areas that are already under tension due to movements in the earth's crust.

Major earthquake zones
Areas experiencing frequent earthquakes

WHAT IS A SEISMOGRAPH?

FACT FILE

The edges of the Pacific plate are surrounded by earthquakes, volcanic activity, and hot springs, caused by the crust shifts and hot lava rising near the surface.

Earthquakes occur all over the world. Although you don't always feel the earth shaking, scientists can make accurate records of the earthquakes from anywhere in the world. Special instruments, called *seismographs*, allow them to do this. The study of earthquakes is known as *seismology*. The seismograph picks up signals that are caused by one rock mass rubbing against another. The energy produced causes vibrations in the rocks. These vibrations can travel thousands of miles and still be felt.

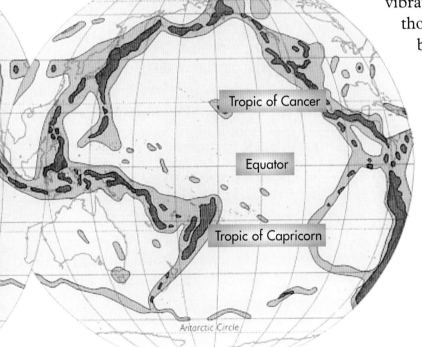

Arctic Circle

Tropic of Cancer

Equator

Tropic of Capricorn

Antarctic Circle

Different types of volcanic eruption

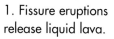

1. Fissure eruptions release liquid lava.

2. In Hawaiian eruptions, the lava is less fluid and produces short domes.

3. Vulcanian eruptions are more violent and eject solid lava.

WHEN ARE VOLCANOES DORMANT?

FACT FILE

A major volcanic eruption can hurl boulders high into the air. These boulders, called *volcanic bombs*, can be very large.

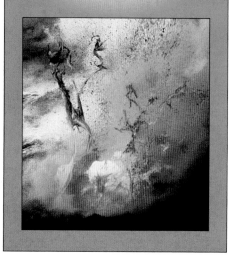

The word *dormant* actually means *sleeping*. So, when people talk about a volcano being dormant, it really means that the volcano is temporarily sleeping and could erupt at any time in the future. An extinct volcano, on the other hand, is one that will not become active again. Like earthquakes, volcanoes mainly occur along fault lines. Molten rock, gases, and ash are forced out through a gap in the earth's crust, releasing pressure that has built up. When there is very little pressure, the volcano can remain in a dormant state for many years. On the island of Maui, there is a volcano called *Haleakala*, which rises to a height of about 10,025 feet. It is the world's largest inactive volcano. Its crater is about 20 miles around and 2,720 feet deep.

4. Strombolian eruptions blow out incandescent material.

5. In the Peléean type, a blocked vent is cleared explosively.

6. A Plinian eruption is a continuous blast of gas that rises to immense heights.

WHEN WAS THE LARGEST VOLCANIC ERUPTION?

The island of Krakatau (west of Java) in Indonesia was a small volcanic island. The volcano had laid dormant for over 200 years, until August 1883. On May 20, one of the cones erupted violently, and three months later the whole island blew up. It was the biggest explosion in recorded history. For two and a half days, the island was in total darkness because of the amount of dust in the air. A cloud of ash rose 50 miles into the air. The eruption caused a tidal wave that killed 36,000 people. The explosion could be heard and felt in Australia, 2,200 miles away.

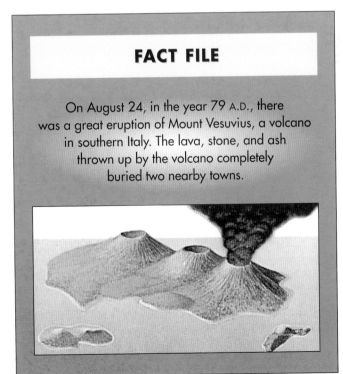

FACT FILE

On August 24, in the year 79 A.D., there was a great eruption of Mount Vesuvius, a volcano in southern Italy. The lava, stone, and ash thrown up by the volcano completely buried two nearby towns.

HOW ARE MOUNTAINS FORMED?

Mountains can be formed in three different ways. Volcanic mountains form when lava from deep inside the earth cools and hardens on the surface.

Other mountains form when two plates move toward each other under pressure or when an oceanic plate is pushed under a continental crust. The pressure causes the ground near the joining plate margins to fault and fold. The ground is forced upward to form mountains. The Rockies, Alps, Andes, Urals, and Himalayas were all formed in this way.

The earth's crust can also fracture and create faults, which means that large blocks of land can be moved upward or downward. Faults in the rocks normally occur when there is a lot of pressure on the rocks. Mountain building is a slow process that happens over centuries.

FACT FILE

Rockslides are common where forests have been destroyed on mountainsides. There are no longer any tree roots to stabilize the loose material.

Three ways in which a mountain can form

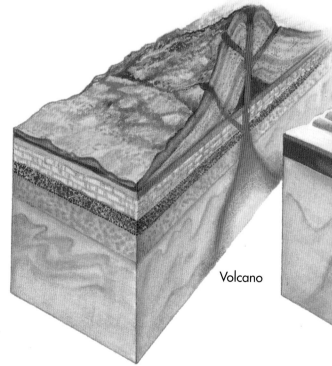

Volcano

WHEN WAS THE TOP OF MOUNT EVEREST FIRST REACHED?

FACT FILE

Mountain peaks are often seen to be surrounded by layers of clouds. This is because when winds laden with water are blown toward the mountains, they are forced to rise and the temperature drops. The water condenses into clouds at these higher altitudes.

Mount Everest in the Himalayas is 5.5 miles high. At these altitudes, mountains are constantly covered in snow and ice, and there is little oxygen to breathe. Mount Everest was conquered on May 29, 1953, when a Nepalese guide, Tenzing Norgay, and a New Zealander, Edmund Hillary, reached the highest point on the earth's surface. Since then, many people have climbed Mount Everest, and all the world's major peaks have now been conquered.

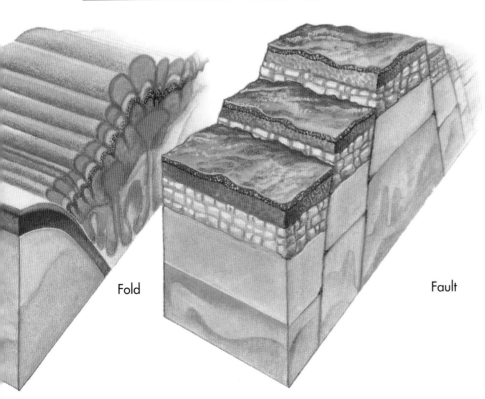

Fold

Fault

WHAT IS A MONSOON?

A monsoon is a season of very heavy rain falling in tropical countries. Monsoons are most common near the equator. They occur when seasonal winds spring up carrying moist air from the sea. Important crops, such as rice, depend on the monsoon season to provide the right growing conditions.

If the monsoon rains fail, famine commonly follows. There are also special winds called *monsoon winds*. These winds change their direction with the season. In India, the monsoon winds blow south as hot, dry winds in the wintertime. They blow north in the summer, bringing heavy rainfall.

Mist over high ground

FACT FILE

The Aborigines believe that if a possum is left cooking by the water's edge, a sizzling sound is produced. This noise irritates the rainbow snake, who they believe crawls underground towards the source of the noise. As the snake moves along, the weather turns stormy, and the monsoon rains begin.

WHEN DO FOG AND MIST OCCUR?

FACT FILE

Fog particles are small, less than 1/25,000 of an inch in diameter. When there is dense fog, it is because there may be as many as 20,000 of these particles in one cubic inch of air.

Tiny water droplets condensing from moist air cause fog and mist to rise. These water droplets can occur at ground level. The air can only hold a limited amount of water. If the air suddenly cools, its capacity to hold water is reduced, which results in a mist or fog.

When fog occurs, visibility can be severely affected. Mist is less dense. It commonly occurs on calm, clear nights when heat rises, forming a thin layer of mist close to the ground. Mist often forms over water when a mass of warm air passes over a cold stretch of water.

Sometimes, visibility is affected in built up areas due to mist and fog, but this is sometimes mistaken for smog. Smog is a buildup of exhaust fumes and factory smoke that hangs over the area until a great amount of air movement can blow the smog away.

WHEN DO WE SEE MIRAGES?

Mirages form in hot deserts where the air is so hot that it bends and distorts light rays. The shimmering images that a mirage produces have often tricked travelers in deserts. People think that they can see an oasis or town on the horizon, but in reality, it is not there.

Under certain conditions, such as desert air heated by intense sunshine, the air rapidly cools with elevation. Therefore, the air increases in density and refractive power. Sunlight reflected downward from the top of an object (for example, the camel above) will be directed through the cool air in the normal way. When the sky is the object of the mirage, the land is mistaken for a lake or sheet of water.

FACT FILE

Deserts are found where there is too little water to allow plant life to grow. Salt deserts form when shallow seas or lakes dry up, leaving a deposit of smooth salt.

WHEN ARE DESERTS COLD?

About one-third of the world's land surface is covered by desert. Not all deserts are hot and arid.

Antarctica is the biggest cold desert in the world. The blanket of 1.2-mile-thick ice covering the Tundra, howling winds, and freezing temperatures stop plants and land-living animals from surviving. But the ocean around this frozen desert is full of fish and krill, so the coasts are home to millions of birds. Once the Antarctic winter sun sets, it is dark for more than two months.

The Gobi desert in Mongolia and western China is also very cold in the winter, with temperatures below freezing. However, the temperature in the summer is hot.

FACT FILE

One of the animals that has survived the Arctic conditions is the polar bear. In very cold climates, an animal needs excellent insulation to keep its body heat from escaping. Animals can have dense hair, fur, feathers, or a thick layer of fat or blubber.

The Tundra

COULD THE SUN STOP SHINING?

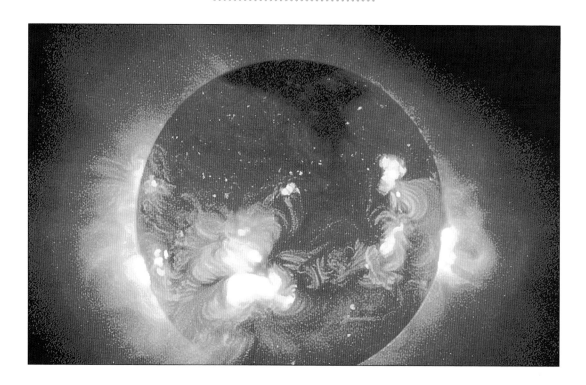

The sun is our nearest star. Stars are massive nuclear reactors generating energy in their cores. It is the heat and light from the sun that makes life on earth possible. The sun is a steady and dependable object in the sky. Whether we can see it or not, we know that it is always there. To answer the question–the sun will never stop shining.

As the earth spins on its axis, the sun shines on one side of it, giving us daylight. The sun is not visible during a solar eclipse. This is when the moon blocks the sun's light from reaching the earth, so that the sun seems to disappear.

FACT FILE

The direction of the earth's rotation means that the sun appears to rise in the east and set in the west. The earth rotates towards the east, so the sun is first visible from that direction.

WHEN WAS THE LONGEST HEAT WAVE?

The longest heat wave ever recorded occured in Marble Bar, Australia, when the temperature stayed above 100°F for 162 days. It lasted from October 23, 1923, to April 7, 1924.

The highest mean annual temperature recorded is 93.9°F in Dallol, Ethiopia. The lowest recorded temperature (outside of the poles) was –90°F in Verkhoyansk, Siberia, on February 6, 1933. The lowest mean annual temperature of –69.9°F was recorded at the Plateau Station, in Antarctica.

FACT FILE

Some living things have adapted to survive long periods of time without water. Plants, such as cacti, have the ability to conserve water. They also minimize water loss as they have no leaves, and photosynthesis takes place in the stem. They have roots that reach deep into the ground for water.

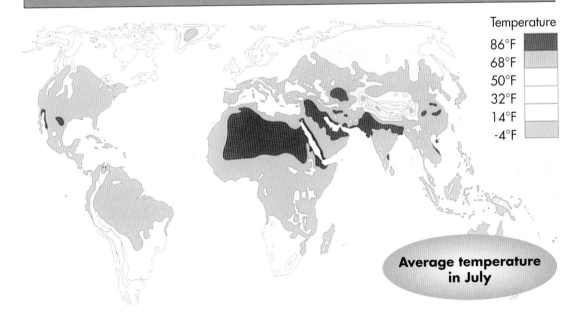

Temperature

86°F	
68°F	
50°F	
32°F	
14°F	
-4°F	

Average temperature in July

HOW DOES WATER BECOME SALTY?

FACT FILE

Lighthouses were built to warn ships at sea that they were approaching land and rocky water. Their beam of light across the waves made traveling by boat much safer.

Water becomes salty when minerals (including salts) dissolve in it. This process begins when rainwater falls on the land and erodes rock. The minerals in rock are dissolved into the rainwater.

These dissolved minerals in the rainwater enter streams and rivers, gradually working their way into the seas and oceans.

This is a process that is constantly taking place, so the level and concentration of salt in the oceans and seas is always increasing. Some of the minerals are consumed by organisms in the water, but the vast majority of them constitute the saltiness of the water.

WHEN WAS THE LONGEST DROUGHT?

The longest drought in recorded history took place in Calama in the Atacama desert of northern Chile. For four centuries, beginning in 1571, no rain fell in the area. It was not until 1971 that rainfall was first recorded again. The Atacama desert, which lies between the Andes and the Pacific ocean, is recognized as the driest place in the world.

The Atacama desert remains so dry because it lies in a region where there is constant high air pressure, with little air movement and with few clouds overhead.

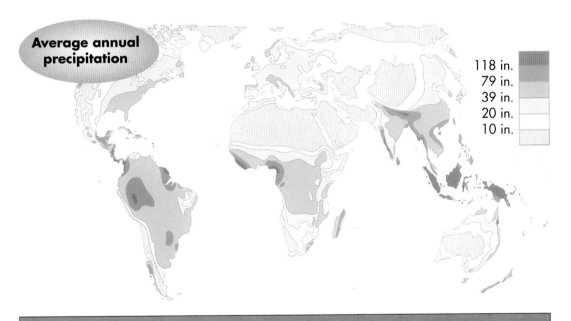

Average annual precipitation

118 in.
79 in.
39 in.
20 in.
10 in.

FACT FILE

Some people believe that animals are good predictors of weather. One such belief is that if cows are standing in their field, dry weather is expected. If they are lying down, however, rain is expected.

WHEN DOES WATER TURN INTO SNOW?

Water turns into snow at temperatures below 32°F. Snow forms when water in clouds freezes into tiny ice crystals. This moist air freezes around tiny dust particles or chemical substances floating in the clouds. These particles become the core, or the nucleus, of each crystal. Snow crystals grow in size when more water crystallizes around a particular nucleus. This happens more if the air is humid.

Snowflakes are formed when a number of crystals join together in a cluster. The structure of snowflakes is often a beautiful, hexagonal form. It is believed that no two snowflakes are identical. These fall from the clouds onto land as snow.

FACT FILE

Eskimos live in houses, called *igloos*, made completely of snow. The Eskimos cut away blocks of snow and build the igloo as though they are using bricks. Because the air is so cold where they are built, the igloos do not melt.

WHY DOES THE SNOW LINE MOVE?

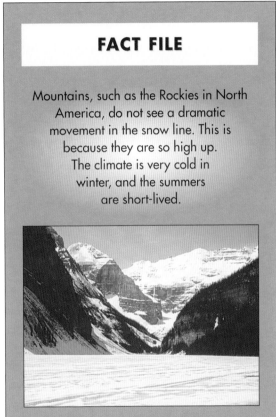

FACT FILE

Mountains, such as the Rockies in North America, do not see a dramatic movement in the snow line. This is because they are so high up. The climate is very cold in winter, and the summers are short-lived.

Snow lines are clearly visible on mountains. They mark the area where a mountain is permanently covered in snow.

The highest points of a mountain are much colder than the lower points. The snow that falls on the higher regions never thaws because it is so cold. In the summer, however, the warmer weather begins to melt some of the snow. This causes the snow line to move up the mountain.

As the summer months pass and the winter months return, the snow line moves further down the mountain again.

In colder regions, the snow line is close to ground level. Where the air is warmer, the snow line is closer to the top of the mountain.

WHEN WAS THE EARTH FORMED?

No one knows exactly when the earth was formed. However, scientists have reasoned that it probably formed about 6,000 million years ago. This figure is twice as long as when the first signs of life are believed to have appeared on earth, about 3,000 million years ago.

One scientific theory for the creation of the earth is that it began as a huge ball of hot gases, which cooled to form the planet. Seas of dissolved chemicals covered the land, and the air was an atmosphere of different gases. The atmosphere was thought to have consisted of swirling gaseous clouds, which most likely caused huge electrical storms.

The poisonous gases in the atmosphere must have reacted to produce oxygen, which triggered off the first beginnings of life on earth.

FACT FILE

As earth cooled down, it gave off clouds of steam and gas. The moisture in these clouds eventually turned to rain, which formed the first seas.

WHEN WAS THE MEDITERRANEAN A DRY BASIN?

We know the Mediterranean Sea today as a huge body of water off the coast of Europe. However, it was not always like that.

Approximately 5 million years ago, the Mediterranean Sea was a dry basin. Movements in the earth's crust opened up the Gibraltar Straits between the continental areas that are now Africa and Europe. The Atlantic Ocean would have poured through this new opening into the dry basin. The result was an enormous waterfall, nearly half a mile high. So much water poured in from the Atlantic that the Mediterranean Sea was created in only a few years.

FACT FILE

Of course, through time, the shape of the continents will continue to change, and new seas will form. Some seas might even join together. Below is what the earth might look like in the future.

150 million years from now

Present day

HOW MANY PARTS DOES THE EARTH HAVE ?

The earth consists of five parts: the first, the atmosphere, is gaseous; the second, the hydrosphere, is liquid; the third, fourth, and fifth, the lithosphere, mantle, and core, are mostly solid. The atmosphere is the gaseous envelope that surrounds the solid body of the planet. Although it is more than 700 miles (1100 km) thick, about half of its mass is concentrated in the lower 3.5 miles (5.6 km). The lithosphere, consisting mainly of the cold, rigid, rocky crust of the earth, extends to depths of 60 miles (100 km). The hydrosphere is the layer of water that covers approximately 70.8 percent of the surface of the earth. The mantle and core are the heavy interior of the earth, making up most of the earth's mass.

FACT FILE

The earth's inner core is made up mostly of iron and nickel. It is 850 miles (1,370 km.) deep and is thought to have a temperature of around 8,100°F.

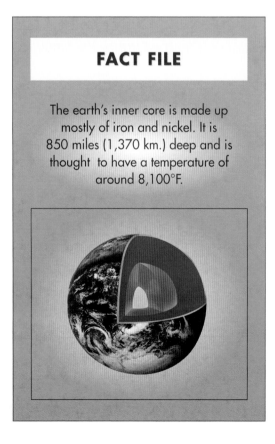

WHAT IS PANGAEA?

It is thought that about 225 million years ago all of the world's land masses were joined together into one supercontinent, called *Pangaea*, surrounded by a single universal sea, Panthalassa. Through the upheavals of plate tectonics, the shifting of the earth's crust tore the supercontinent apart during the middle of the Mesozoic period. As a result, large bodies of land drifted across the surface of the earth to ultimately become our present-day continents. It is now believed that several moving plates of the earth's crust were formed by volcanic activity. The clues to the movement of the earth's surface can only be found on the present-day continents in rocks, fossils, and structures that appear older than 200 million years.

FACT FILE

As a result of Pangaea breaking apart, certain species of terrestrial mammals became isolated in Antarctica, South America, Africa, and Australia. It was thousands of years before a volcanic eruption would reunite South and North America with a land bridge.

HOW IS MINING PERFORMED?

The earliest forms of mining involved following seams of metal in tunnels that were driven into rock. This method is still in use today, usually in deep mines where other techniques would be impossible. Tunnels are made by explosives and automatic machines. Some of these mines go thousands of feet into the rock face, where it can be very hot and dangerous.

Today, we mine minerals, diamonds, metals, coal, and rock for building material. Placer mining uses huge floating dredgers to extract metals. Strip mining is used to obtain coal and minerals that lie close to the surface. Open pit mining involves blasting into rock to produce a huge quarry from which material is removed layer by layer.

FACT FILE

The metals that are used to make coins come from mines. Pure metals (those not mixed with other substances) are called *noble metals*, and these include gold, silver, platinum, and copper.

HOW DOES COAL FORM?

FACT FILE

Before we had central heating to warm our houses, most people had coal fires. Matches were a quick and easy way to light them.

Coal is formed from the compressed remains of plants that lived in bogs 250–350 million years ago. This was during the Carboniferous Period, when primitive animals first appeared on the land. Coal formed from the remains of tree ferns and other primitive trees, which were covered with mud and sand and buried as new rock was laid down. Very gradually, over millions of years, this material turned into coal.

A similar process is taking place today in peat bogs, where the rotting remains of heather form peat. When the peat is dried, it burns in a similar way as coal. In some parts of the world, a soft shale, called *brown coal*, is mined. The hardest and purest form of coal is called *anthracite*.

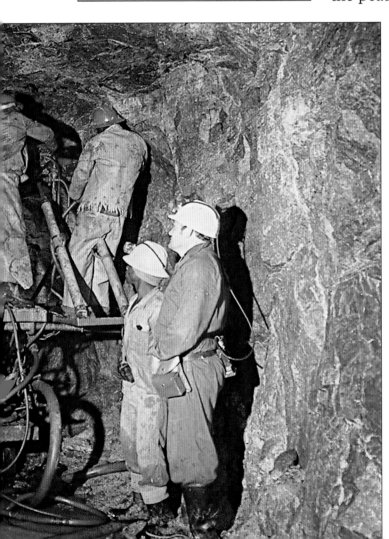

HOW DO GEYSERS GET SO HOT?

Most of the water in a geyser originates from rain or snow, which gathers in underground reservoirs acting like storage basins. These reservoirs are connected to the surface by a tube.

The rock further down inside the earth is extremely hot. Steam-like gasses from the rocks rise up through cracks, heating the water in the reservoirs to boiling temperatures. When a combination of steam and water rises freely from the depths, a continuously boiling hot spring is created.

Geysers are created when the tube or passageway is not straight, as is often the case. It erupts onto the surface as the water is converted into steam. Because steam needs more space than water, as this eruption takes place, it pushes up through the channel of water above it, making an explosive ejection of steam into the air.

FACT FILE

This hotel heats the water in its pool. The pool is a luxury attraction, and people have always enjoyed swimming in warm water.

AT WHAT TEMPERATURE DOES WATER BOIL?

As a liquid is heated, it begins to change to a gas at a certain point. The vapor is called *steam*. Steam occurs because the molecules in liquid move faster at high temperatures, until they escape into the air. Light molecules escape more easily than heavy molecules, which means that heavy, thick liquids only boil at extremely high temperatures.

The boiling point of a liquid depends on the air pressure. The pressure becomes lower at altitude, so high up on a mountain slope, water boils at a much lower temperature than normal. Water boils at 212°F at sea level but at only 162°F at an altitude of 1.9 miles.

When water boils, the steam it produces is not visible while the water remains at boiling point. But as the steam cools, it forms tiny droplets of water, making it look cloudy. This is what you see when you breath outside in very cold temperatures.

FACT FILE

Water exists in even the driest places in the world, such as a desert. It is stored in porous rock and sand. Sometimes, the edges of these water deposits are exposed, and an oasis is formed where plants grow and animals live.

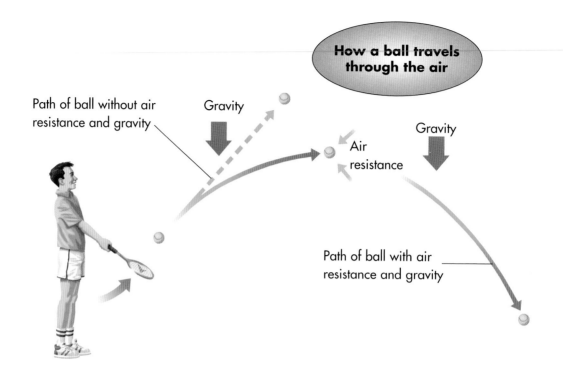

How a ball travels through the air

Path of ball without air resistance and gravity

Gravity

Gravity

Air resistance

Path of ball with air resistance and gravity

WHAT IS GRAVITY?

Gravity is the force that pulls towards the center of the earth. It doesn't matter where you stand on the earth's surface, the ground is always "down" or below you.

The force of gravity depends on the mass, or amount of material, of an object. Objects only feel heavy because of their mass.

Sir Issac Newton realized that gravity not only affects the earth, but it also controls the movement of the planets and the stars, as well as the orbit of the moon around the earth. When you whirl something around your head on the end of a piece of string, it flies outwards and appears to defy the force of gravity. This is called *centrifugal force*. When you let go of the string, the centrifugal force makes the object fly away in a straight line.

FACT FILE

Sir Isaac Newton (1643–1727) was the first scientist to develop the laws of gravity. It is said he was inspired by seeing an apple fall from a tree.

WHEN DOES LIGHTNING STRIKE?

To understand exactly what lightning is, we must recall a fact we know about electricity. We know that things become electrically charged–either positively or negatively. A positive charge has a great attraction for a negative charge. As the charges become greater, this attraction becomes stronger. A point is finally reached where the strain of being kept apart becomes too great for the charges. A discharge takes place to relieve the strain and make the two bodies electrically equal. This is exactly what

happens in the case of lightning. This discharge follows the path that offers the least resistance. That is the reason why lightning often zigzags. Moist air is only a fair conductor of electricity. That is why lightning often stops when it starts raining.

FACT FILE

The electrical nature of the nervous system was discovered after Italian scientist Galvani noticed that frogs' legs twitched when an electrical current was applied to the nerve.

WHEN WAS LIGHTNING FIRST UNDERSTOOD?

Ben Franklin (1706–1790) was an American with many talents. He was a printer, scientist, and politician who played an important part in founding the United States.

He discovered the nature of lightning while flying a kite during a thunderstorm. Franklin noticed sparks jumping from a key tied to the end of the wet string. This could very easily have killed him, but luckily, it did not. He went on to invent the lightning conductor, a strip of copper that is run from the top of a building to the ground so that lightning can reach the earth safely.

Lightning is a significant weather hazard and occurs at an average rate of 50 to 100 discharges per second. Lightning rods and metallic conductors can be used to protect a structure by intercepting and diverting the lightning current into the ground. When lightning is likely to occur, people are advised to stay indoors, in a car, away from open doors and windows, and to avoid contact with any electrical appliances or plumbing that might be exposed to the outside environment.

FACT FILE

A lightning conductor is a metal rod that is placed so that it points upward above the highest point of a tall building. If lightning does strike the building, it is the conductor, not the building itself, that the spark hits.

HOW DO WE SEE THE SPECTRUM OF LIGHT?

Sir Isaac Newton

FACT FILE

Sir Isaac Newton used his discoveries about light to build a new kind of telescope. It used a reflecting mirror instead of a glass lense to magnify images.

Sir Isaac Newton of Cambridge University first discovered the secrets of how light is divided up. We think of ordinary light as being white, but really light is a mixture of red, orange, yellow, green, blue, and violet colors. When sunlight strikes the beveled edge of a mirror, a glass prism, or the surface of a soap bubble, we can see the different hues in light. What actually happens is that the white light is broken up into the different wave lengths that are seen by our eyes. These wave lengths form a band of parallel stripes, each hue grading into the one next to it. This band is called a *spectrum*. In a spectrum, the red line is always at one end, and the blue and violet lines are at the other.

THE NATURAL

WORLD

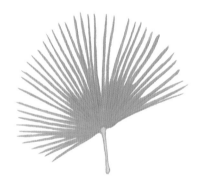

CONTENTS

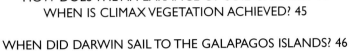

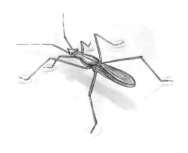

HOW DOES THE APPEARANCE OF SOIL CHANGE?

Soil changes its appearance when the biological or chemical make-up of it varies. For example, red soil is found in areas where there is a high content of iron compounds. Oxisol is a good example of this. It is found in tropical regions where both chemical and biological activity are high. It is illustrated in picture 5 below.

The illustrations below show different types of soils. You can see that their appearances change enormously. Picture 1 is tundra soil, which is very dark and peaty. Picture 2 is soil belonging to desert regions. These areas tend to be unsuitable for plant growth, so this soil is lacking in nutrients and organic matter. The light-brown soils in pictures 3 and 4 are common in grassland areas. In contrast, soils 6, 7, 8, and 9 are typical of northern climates, where there is heavy rainfall and slow evaporation. These richer soils are suitable for abundant plant growth.

Different types of soil

FACT FILE

Soil is not just a single, consistent layer of material. Below the surface, there are different parts to soil, as shown below.

humus
topsoil
subsoil
fragmented rock
solid rock

WHEN IS CLIMAX VEGETATION ACHIEVED?

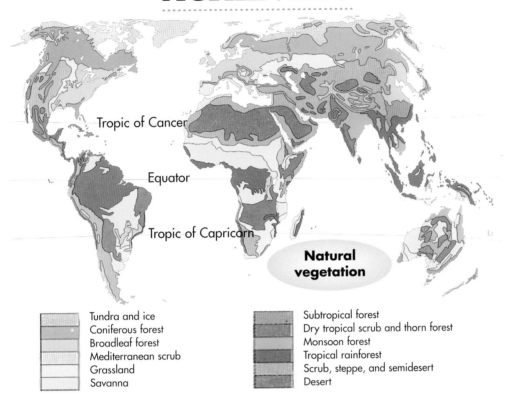

Tropic of Cancer

Equator

Tropic of Capricorn

Natural vegetation

Tundra and ice
Coniferous forest
Broadleaf forest
Mediterranean scrub
Grassland
Savanna

Subtropical forest
Dry tropical scrub and thorn forest
Monsoon forest
Tropical rainforest
Scrub, steppe, and semidesert
Desert

When vegetation first starts growing in newly formed soil, it is at a disadvantage because the soil will not be nutrient-rich. As the plants die, they enrich the soil, allowing more plants to grow. As the soil gets older, it has gleaned more and more nutrients from dead plants, and more and more plants are able to grow successfully in the soil. Climax vegetation occurs when the vegetation is totally suited to the soil in the given climate. In reality, this can never last permanently because of the ever-changing environment.

FACT FILE

Rainforests have developed in areas where the soil is very fertile and where there is a great deal of rainfall. The varied vegetation suggests the soil is extremely nutrient-rich.

WHEN DID DARWIN SAIL TO THE GALAPAGOS ISLANDS?

The marine iguana

In 1831, Charles Darwin (1809–1882) set out on an exploratory voyage in the ship *Beagle*, heading for South America. The voyage lasted five years. During this time, Darwin kept careful notes of everything he saw. In particular, he noted the strange animal life on the Galapagos Islands, off the western coast of Ecuador. He was disturbed by the fact that the birds and tortoises of the Galapagos Islands tended to resemble species found on the nearby continent, while inhabits of similar adjoining islands to the Galapagos had quite different animal populations. In London, Darwin later learned that the finches he had brought back belonged to a different species, not merely different varieties, as he had originally believed.

FACT FILE

When Charles Darwin first published his theories on evolution, they created a sensation. It took a while before they were accepted.

WHEN DID DARWIN PUBLISH *THE ORIGIN OF THE SPECIES?*

A Galapagos-dwelling tortoise

Upon his return from the voyage to Galapagos, Darwin turned over all the specimens he had brought back to cataloging experts in Cambridge and London. In South America, he had found fossils of extinct armadillos that were similar but not identical to the living animals he had seen. On November 24, 1859, Darwin published his theories in a book called *The Origin of the Species*. The book caused a great sensation, but it was some time before it was accepted by the scientific world. The first edition sold out immediately, and by 1872, the work had run through six editions. It became generally accepted that evolution took place similar to how Darwin suggested.

FACT FILE

We can see how evolution has changed living things by examining fossils. Fossils preserve the body parts of living creatures from long ago so that we can see how they have changed over millions of years.

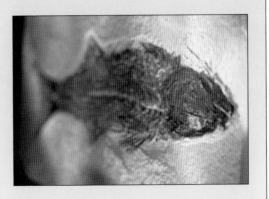

Carl Linnaeus

WHY DID LINNAEUS DEVELOP A CLASSIFICATION SYSTEM?

Carl Linnaeus (1707–1778) was a Swedish botanist and explorer who was the first to create a uniform system for naming plants and animals. Most plants and animals have popular names that vary from place to place. Scientific names are given so that the same name is recognized by people everywhere. Latin is the language used for scientific names. The scientific names are in two parts. The first is the generic name, which describes a group of related living things, and the second name is the specific name, which applies to only that living thing.

FACT FILE

The Latin name of the White Water Lily is *Nymphaea alba*. They are one of a group of plants whose flowers close up at night.

WHEN IS AN ANIMAL A VERTEBRATE?

An animal is classified as a vertebrate if it has a backbone that provides support for its muscles and protection for its spinal cord. Vertebrates include fish, amphibians, reptiles, birds, and mammals. The backbone is actually a series of small bones called *vertebrae*. They are joined together and locked with ropelike ligaments to provide a flexible but extremely strong anchor for the back muscles. The spinal cord runs down a channel inside the vertebrae, providing protection from injury. Some primitive fish, such as sharks and rays, have a spine made of a tough rubbery material called *cartilage*. There are approximately 45,000 living species of vertebrates. In size, they range from tiny fishes to elephants and whales (of up to 100 tons), the largest animals ever to have existed. They are adapted to life underground, on the earth, and in the air.

FACT FILE

The duck-billed platypus is a very unusual, small, semiaquatic mammal. It lives in the lakes and streams of eastern Australia and Tasmania. It is notable for having a broad, flat, rubbery snout, webbed feet, and for laying eggs.

WHAT IS MIGRATION?

Migration is the mass movement of groups of animals or birds. It is caused by the need to find food, by climatic changes during the year, and by the need to breed. Every autumn, for example, swallows gather in large flocks to rest before they begin their long migration to Africa. Swallows and their relatives, swifts and martins, all migrate to Africa when the weather becomes too cold for them to catch their insect prey. They return in the spring when the weather in northern Europe warms up. The Arctic tern makes the longest-known migration of any bird. It travels from the Arctic to the Antarctic and then back again. On its flight, it passes through Japan, Alaska, Canada, and Fiji before returning home again to breed.

FACT FILE

Many fish migrate in both fresh water and the ocean. Tuna make some of the longest migrations. They migrate because of sea temperature, as fish need the correct temperature in order to breed.

WHEN DOES A CYGNET BECOME A SWAN?

FACT FILE

In captivity, geese and swans have been known to live for more than 30 years. There are reports of geese exceeding 40 years of age. With luck, a wild swan may survive for 15 to 20 years.

Young swans, or cygnets, are hatched with a complete covering of down. They can take to the water as soon as they leave the nest, which is within 24 to 48 hours. Right from the start, they are able to find food for themselves. At least one parent remains with them, guarding, guiding, and initially protecting them at night. Their dark downy plumage is retained for two to six weeks and is then replaced gradually by juvenile feathers. The flight feathers are the last to develop, taking from five weeks to five months. By the age of six months, the cygnets are practically indistinguishable from adults in plumage and in size.

WHY DO ANIMALS BECOME EXTINCT?

GIANT PANDA: less than 1,000 remain

YELLOW-EYED PENGUIN: about 3,000 remain in the wild

RED WOLF: only 200 remain in captivity, none in the wild

According to the theory of evolution, some animal species become extinct because they are less successful than other species that gradually replace them.

These so-called "failed" animals are also unable to adapt to changing circumstances. Human beings have sped up their extinction by changing the environment so rapidly that animals do not have the time to adapt. For example, the destruction of Indonesian rainforests has left nowhere for the orangutan to live. It would take millions of years for the animal to evolve into a ground-living creature. Hunting is the main reason for the reduced numbers and probable extinction of animals such as the tiger, the blue whale, and the giant panda.

FACT FILE

The number of black rhinos has been reduced to about 2,550 due to poaching. Most of the ones that survive today live in protected game parks.

WHY DO AMPHIBIANS LEAVE THE WATER?

Although frogs and toads can live on land, they have to return to the water to breed. Common frogs can be found in many freshwater habitats. They often show up in garden ponds, lakes, canals, and pools.

FACT FILE

A frog's eyes are on top of its head so it can see above the water's surface. This way it is able to keep a watch out for predators.

Toads usually live in wooded ponds and lakes and are sometimes seen in pools.

Frogs and toads are amphibians, which means that they are equally at home on land and in water. Toads, however, spend more time away from water than most frogs. Their skin is leathery and warty, and they do not lose water so easily on dry land. On land, a frog hops to escape danger, whereas a toad will walk. The bodies of some frogs and toads have adapted to survive in very dry conditions, such as in deserts.

WHEN DID THE FIRST PLANTS APPEAR?

Plants are organisms that use light as a source of energy to produce the food they need in order to live and grow. The earth's original atmosphere contained poisonous gases. The lack of oxygen meant that no animals or plants could survive on the earth. The earliest plants or plant-like bacteria began the process of photosynthesis, which releases oxygen and a waste product. This gas gradually built up in the atmosphere as the plant life spread, making it possible for oxygen-dependent animals to evolve.

Coral was formed by bacteria in much the same way as plants. It is made up of a variety of invertebrate marine organisms of a stonelike, horny, or leathery consistency. They live in colonies begun by just one polyp. Each polyp builds a hard skeleton around itself.

Coral reef

FACT FILE

Lichens are a mixture of algae and fungi. Many grow like a mat over rocks or tree trunks, while others look like small branched plants.

WHEN DO TREES STOP GROWING?

Californian giant redwood

The simple answer to this question is that trees never stop growing. Trees are the largest living organisms on earth. The largest tree of all is the Californian giant redwood, which can grow nearly 330 feet tall and can have a trunk that is 36 feet thick. The oldest-known trees are bristlecone pine trees. They grow in the White Mountains in California. Although they are quite small, some of these gnarled trees are more than 4,500 years old.

Environmental factors, such as water availability, soil quality, and change in the weather, can affect the growth of a tree. Water is pulled up from the roots to the top of the tree by their leaves.

FACT FILE

Bonsai trees are decorative miniature trees that were first developed in Japan. They are grown in shallow dishes, and the shoots and roots are carefully trimmed to stunt their growth. They can live for hundreds of years.

WHEN ARE SEEDS FORMED?

The main way flowering plants reproduce and spread is through seeds. After the plant has been fertilized, the egg cell develops into a seed from which a new plant develops. The seed contains an embryo from which the new plant grows. It also contains a food store to nourish the embryo until it has developed roots and leaves. The seed is enclosed in a tough outer coating to protect it from drying out. Many seeds are carried by the wind. Some even have a fluffy umbrella (like the dandelion seed head above), which enables them to be carried for very long distances.

FACT FILE

The biggest seed is the coco de mer, a kind of coconut that grows in the Seychelles, a group of islands in the Indian Ocean. The coco de mer seeds weigh 50 pounds each.

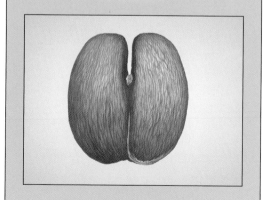

WHEN DOES POLLINATION TAKE PLACE?

FACT FILE

The flowers of orchids are highly specialized for pollination by insects. When the insect pushes into the flower to reach the nectar, the pollen sticks onto its head.

Pollination is the process of transferring pollen from the stamen to the stigma. It is possible for flowers to pollinate themselves or other flowers on the same plant. This is called *self-pollination*. It is, however, much better for the health of the species if cross-pollination occurs, i.e. pollen is transferred from one plant to another. The most common method involves insects that are attracted to the flowers for their nectar. Pollen grains stick to the insects' bodies and are effectively transferred from one plant to another as the insect moves from flower to flower. Other less attractive types of flower use wind to transport their pollen.

WHEN DO TREES LOSE THEIR LEAVES?

A tree that loses its leaves in winter is called a *deciduous tree*. Trees that are about to lose their leaves in the autumn conserve their food supplies by withdrawing all the nutrients from the leaves. Chlorophyll is broken down in the leaves, causing their pigment to change. Eventually, all the nutrients are moved from the leaves, and they wither, turn brown, and eventually fall from the tree.

FACT FILE

Every year a tree grows, it deposits a new layer of cells on the outside of its trunk, beneath the bark. This new layer is called an *annual ring*. Counting the annual rings will tell you the exact age of a tree.

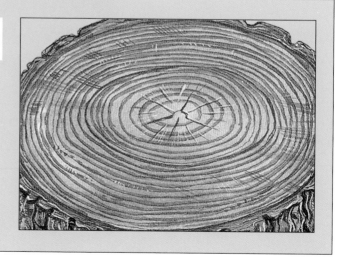

HOW CAN PLANTS EAT INSECTS?

Venus flytrap

FACT FILE

Some insects use camouflage to blend into their environment, protecting themselves from predators.

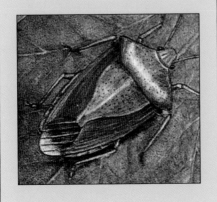

Plants growing in some areas need to supplement their food supply by catching insects. Bog water contains very little nitrogen, but some bog plants can obtain this substance by catching and digesting insects. They are known as insectivorous plants. Other insectivorous plants are covered with sticky tentacles that trap flies. The most remarkable is the Venus flytrap. This plant has two clawed plates that slam together when an insect walks over them and touches a trigger hair. Other insect-eating plants are aquatic, catching tiny crustaceans in bladder-shaped underwater traps. Some of the largest insectivorous plants live in the tropical rainforests.

HOW DO CATERPILLARS TURN INTO BUTTERFLIES?

Young insects develop in two main ways. Butterflies, bees, and beetles go through a process called *metamorphosis*. This means that their eggs hatch into larvae or caterpillars. Later, these become a pupa or chrysalis, within which an adult insect develops. The larvae may live in a different habitat from the adult and require different foods. In species such as grasshoppers and locusts, the young that hatch from eggs look like small adults and are called *nymphs*. As they grow, the nymphs shed their skins, looking more and more like adults each time.

FACT FILE

The wings of a bee or wasp can beat as quickly as 250 times per second during flight. The wing of midges can beat as quickly as 1,000 times per second—which accounts for the high-pitched whine that these tiny insects make.

WHAT DO DRAGONFLIES EAT?

Dragonflies are insects with two pairs of powerful clear wings that enable them to catch insects. They have large eyes for spotting their prey. Dragonfly nymphs live in water, and so, the adults are usually seen near ponds, rivers, and lakes. Some species have a feeding territory, which they guard from other dragonflies. Their clattering wings can sometimes be heard as they battle. When they mate, most species fly around in tandem before they lay their eggs in the water or among the waterside vegetation. Dragonfly nymphs are active carnivores. They feed on other insects but can catch tadpoles or even small fish. On the underside of the head is a flap called the *mask*. This is armed with sharp jaws and fangs. At rest, it is folded, but it can shoot out to catch its prey.

Male emperor dragonfly

Broad-bodied Libellula

FACT FILE

A dragonfly's eyes are large and give it almost 360° vision. They are sensitive to the slightest movement around them. If you look closely, you will be able to see the individual facets of each eye. Each one contains its own lens. Together, they help form the image seen.

HOW DO BEES MAKE HONEY?

Honey is a bee's food. Bees make honey to store for the whole bee colony. In order to transport honey nectar back to the hive after visiting flowers and drinking it, the bee has a honey sac. This is a bag-type growth located in front of the bee's stomach, divided from the stomach by a special valve.

While the nectar is still in the bee's honey sac, the first stage of making honey occurs. A chemical change takes place in the nectar's sugar. Then, water is removed from the nectar by evaporation, caused by both ventilation and the heat of the beehive.

In fact, the honey has so much water removed from it that it will keep indefinitely when the bee stores it in the honeycombs.

The bee puts the honey in the honeycombs to ripen and to be stored as the future food supply for the colony. Depending on the original source of the nectar, the honey comes in a variety of different appearances and flavors.

FACT FILE

Honey is removed from the hive by various methods. It may be squeezed from the comb by presses, or it may be sold in the combs cut from the hive. Most honey, however, is removed from the combs by a machine known as "a honey extractor."

WHEN DO GLOWWORMS GLOW?

The glowworm is not really a worm at all. It is a firefly in an early stage of development, called the *larval stage*. Most adult fireflies do not eat because they did all their eating when they were larvae. They hide during the daytime among the vegetation. After dark, the female climbs up plant stems, and the top of her abdomen glows. The light from a larva's glowing body attracts tiny flies and mosquitoes for the larva to eat.

The Waitomo Caves in New Zealand house a memorable type of glowworm. Tourists entering the Glowworm Grotto in small boats see thousands of lights on the cave ceiling. The glowworms look like stars in a night sky. If you cough or use a camera flash, the lights instantly go off. But wait quietly for a few minutes and they flicker back on, until the cave-ceiling "sky" is again filled with "stars."

FACT FILE

Woodworm, the larvae of the furniture beetle, cause lots of damage to wood both in buildings and in the wild. The damage is evident from the holes they leave behind.

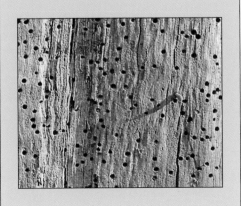

63

HOW DO WATER-DWELLING INSECTS BREATHE?

The saucer bug

Water bugs are found in various types of freshwater habitats. They breathe air and so have to return to the surface of the water from time to time. Ponds and lakes are the best habitats for water bugs. Only a few species live in streams and rivers, except where the current is slow-flowing. Adult water beetles have to breathe air. They do not have gills. Many have a supply of air beneath their wing cases or under their bodies that they renew from time to time. Watch a beetle in a tank. Some species come to the surface tail-first, while a few come to the surface head first.

Adult water beetle

FACT FILE

Place a needle on a sheet of paper in some water. As the paper sinks, the needle floats, showing surface tension. This same process allows the water boatman to "walk" on water. It uses its legs like oars to swim.

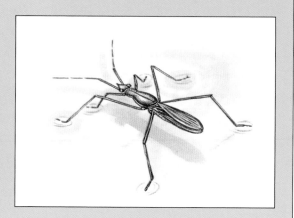

HOW DO DESERT-DWELLING PLANTS GET WATER?

Plants living in very dry regions are specially adapted to not lose too much water. They have smaller leaves, which are often thin and spiny. They may also have no leaves at all, as in the case of the cacti. Because they have no leaves, photosynthesis takes place in the swollen barrel-like stems, which are often covered with protective spines.

Desert plants also conserve water by having a thick, waxy coat over their leaves and stems and by storing water after it rains. Some desert plants have fat, swollen leaves or stems that are filled with water. Desert plants also have extremely long roots that burrow deep into the soil.

FACT FILE

Because plants need to store food and water over the winter or in dry conditions, underground storage organs develop from roots, stems, or leaf bases. We use many of these organs for food.

DISCOVERIES AND

INVENTIONS

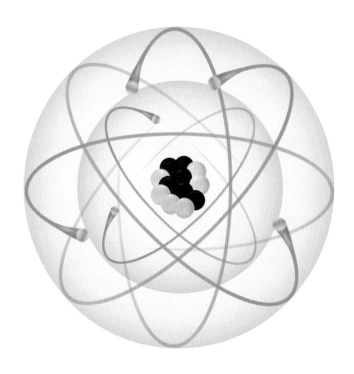

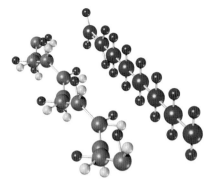

CONTENTS

· ·

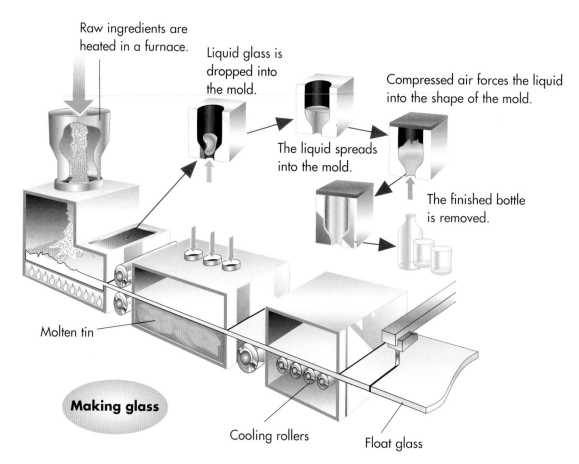

Raw ingredients are heated in a furnace.

Liquid glass is dropped into the mold.

Compressed air forces the liquid into the shape of the mold.

The liquid spreads into the mold.

The finished bottle is removed.

Molten tin

Making glass

Cooling rollers

Float glass

HOW WAS GLASS DISCOVERED?

Glass forms when solid materials are melted and cooled quickly, so that they do not produce crystals. The main ingredients for making glass are sand, soda ash or potash, and lime. They are melted together at a very high temperature. Since these materials are found in abundance all over the world, the secret of glassmaking could have been discovered in many countries.

The Romans were great glassmakers and used glass as a coating for walls. By the time of the Christian era, glass was already being used for windowpanes.

FACT FILE

Mercury is the only metal that is liquid at room temperature. It has a bright, shiny color and flows rapidly when poured. This is why it used to be called *Quicksilver*. It is used today in thermometers and by dentists, who mix it with silver to fill cavities in teeth.

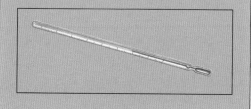

HOW ARE MIRRORS MADE?

FACT FILE

Mirrors are used in lighthouses to reflect light out across the water. The light guides ships at sea.

Mirrors are pieces of glass that have been coated with a reflective material on the back. When a beam of light strikes the surface, none of the light is absorbed. The beam of light is actually reflected back away from the mirror again.

The beam of light is reflected at the exact same angle that it struck the mirror, but in the opposite direction.

Mirrors are used in many ways, such as in telescopes, flashlights, headlights of cars, and lighthouses.

HOW DOES A BATTERY PRODUCE ELECTRICITY?

The electric current that we use for power can be produced in two ways, by big machines known as dynamos and generators and by the portable method of battery cells. Electricity is produced by the the battery cell by changing chemical energy into electrical energy. Some of the chemical energy is converted into heat and the rest into electric current. A battery contains two different conductors, or electrodes. The electrodes are separated by a conducting liquid, called the *electrolyte*. The substances in the battery react chemically with each other to produce an electrical current. As a result of chemical activity, a positive charge builds up at one electrode, and this can flow through a conductor such as a wire, to the other negative electrode.

FACT FILE

An alternative form of power comes from wind farms. Huge windmills are situated on exposed and windy areas to drive dynamos to produce electricity.

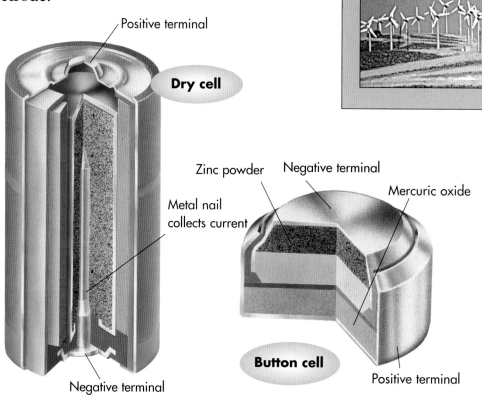

Positive terminal

Dry cell

Zinc powder   Negative terminal

Mercuric oxide

Metal nail collects current

Button cell

Negative terminal

Positive terminal

HOW DOES AN ELECTRIC LIGHT WORK?

Sealed glass bulb

Filament

Metal contact through which current can flow

Some of the earliest experiments leading to the electric lightbulb were conducted by an English scientist, Humphrey Davey. Using a very weak version of what we now call a battery, he connected wire to its end and then attached a piece of carbon to the other end of the wire. Davey found he could produce a sparking light by touching the two pieces of carbon together and then drawing them slightly apart.

Called an *electric arc*, this was the first real evidence that light could be produced by electricity.

In a modern lightbulb, a current is passed through a very thin filament of metal that has a high resistance to the flow of electricity. The filament becomes white-hot and produces light. The bulb contains an inert gas so the filament will not burn.

FACT FILE

Lightning is actually electricity. A huge electrical charge can build up in certain weather conditions. This leads to thunderstorms when bolts of lightning leap between the earth and a cloud. The air is heated to a tremendous temperature, causing the explosive noise of thunder as it suddenly expands.

HOW DO LASERS WORK?

A laser is a device that produces a narrow beam of extremely strong light. Lasers amplify light by causing photons to be bounced back and forth within a substance (which can be a solid, liquid, or gas). This adds extra energy. The result is an intense light emitted in a very narrow beam. The intense beam of light produced by a laser can be used to produce images for publicity or entertainment purposes.

Lasers are used to cut metal and for precision cuts in medical operations. In a CD player, laser light is scanned across the CD's silvery surface, reading the tiny changes in light reflected back. Lasers are also used in office printers and scanners. In engineering, the intense narrow beam of light is used to measure and align roads and tunnels.

FACT FILE

Lasers are used every day in stores and banks. Lasers scan dollar bills to see whether or not they are forgeries. This is done by passing the note under an ultraviolet light.

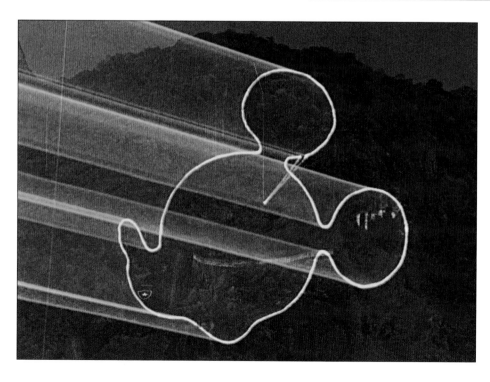

HOW ARE LEVERS USEFUL?

For thousands of years, people have used levers to transfer a force from one place to another and to change the amount of movement that results. Levers are useful when you need to move a heavy object without the use of machinery. To move a heavy object, a long lever can help. The lever is free to move around a point called the *fulcrum*. The shorter end of the lever is placed under the object, and force is applied to the longer end. This will cause the object to be lifted, but the long end of the lever will have to be pushed down a long way to lift the object only a short distance. For example, with a long enough lever, you could lift a car off the ground for a short distance.

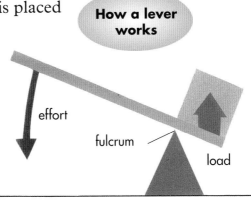

How a lever works

effort

fulcrum

load

FACT FILE

Scissors work with lever action. The cutting blades are worked by putting your forefinger and thumb into the handles and pushing together.

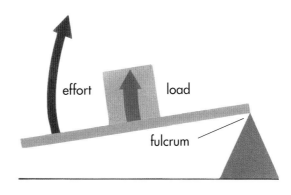

effort

load

fulcrum

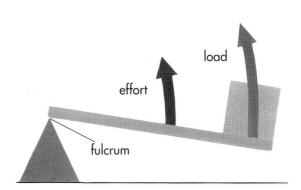

load

effort

fulcrum

HOW DOES SONAR WORK?

Sound waves travel extremely well through water. They are used to detect submarines, wrecks on the seafloor, or by fishermen to find schools of fish. A sonar device under a ship sends out sound waves that travel down through the water. The sound waves are reflected back from any solid object they reach, such as schools of fish or the seafloor.

The echoes are received by the ship and can be used to "draw" an image of the object and its location onto a computer screen.

FACT FILE

Supersonic aircraft actually break the sound barrier. When traveling at such high speeds, aircraft build up a huge wave of compressed air in front of them, causing a sonic "boom."

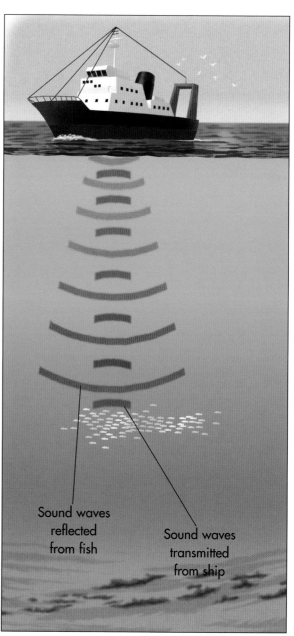

Sound waves reflected from fish

Sound waves transmitted from ship

Sonar, or echo sounding, is used by fishermen to locate schools of fish. It can also be used to detect submarines or to find wrecks on the seafloor.

HOW DO BATS USE SONAR?

Bats use sonar waves to navigate. Bats are nocturnal, which means that they are active at night and sleep during the day. Since bats have to hunt for their food at night, you would imagine that they need exceptionally good eyesight. This is not the case, however, as bats do not depend on their eyes for getting around. When bats fly, they let out a series of very high pitched sounds that are too high to be heard by the human ear.

The echoes from these sounds are thrown back to the bat when it is in flight. It can tell whether the echo came from an obstacle nearby or far away. The bat can then change its course in flight to avoid hitting the obstacle.

Bats produce a continuous high-pitched squeaking noise in flight. The echoes from this sound allow them to navigate in darkness and even to locate small flying insects on which they feed.

Thumb

Arm bone

Five-toed feet

Finger bones

FACT FILE

Musical instruments produce sounds in various ways. But they all cause air to vibrate to carry the sound to your ears. Sounds travel as waves, and it is the shape of the sound wave that determines the kind of sound that will be produced. The pitch of the sound (whether high or low) depends on the frequency of the sound waves.

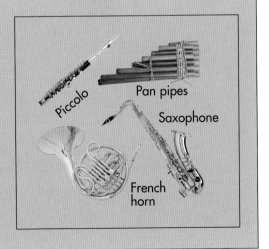

Piccolo

Pan pipes

Saxophone

French horn

HOW DOES A BOAT FLOAT?

When a boat floats on the water's surface, it is the actual fluid that holds it up. The water resists the force of gravity, which otherwise would pull the vessel in a downward direction.

If you take an inflated beach ball into the water, you can feel that the water is "pushing" up the ball, this pressure is *buoyant force* or simply *buoyancy*.

Any solid object placed in liquid pushes the fluid to one side, and if it is less dense than the liquid around it, it will float. Because a boat (or our beach ball) includes a large amount of air, it is less dense than the water. Therefore, it weighs less than the water it has replaced and so floats.

FACT FILE

Helicopters are lifted into the air by their large rotating propellers. Propellers work like narrow wings generating lift as they spin.

Hovercraft are very useful as a means of transportion in shallow waters where conventional boats would run aground. Because they are flat, hovercraft can hold a large number of vehicles.

Air pushing over the upper surface of an aircraft's wing reduces in pressure, allowing higher-pressure air underneath the wing to exert an upward force, thus enabling the airplane to fly.

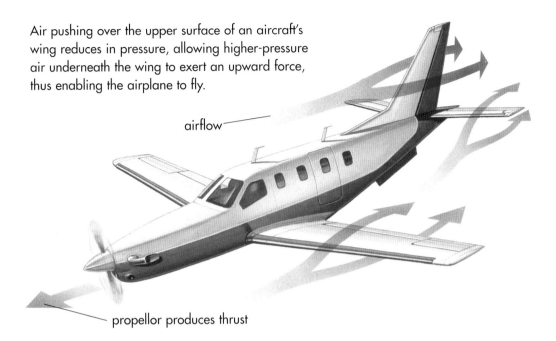

airflow

propellor produces thrust

HOW DO AIRPLANES FLY?

As an airplane moves through the air, air passes over the surface of its wings. These wings are shaped with a curved top surface and a flatter lower surface. This means that air passing over the top of the wing has to travel a little faster than that below the wing. This causes the pressure to lower above the wing, while the air pressure below pushes up. The end result is the lift that keeps the airplane in the air.

The tail surfaces of the airplane keep the wing at the proper angle to provide the right amount of lift. The power to propel the airplane along can come from the engine or in the case of gliders, from rising air currents.

Jet engines propel a plane just like a rocket with a stream of hot gases.

FACT FILE

Leonardo da Vinci (1452–1519) drew his plans for a helicopter hundreds of years before they were even invented.

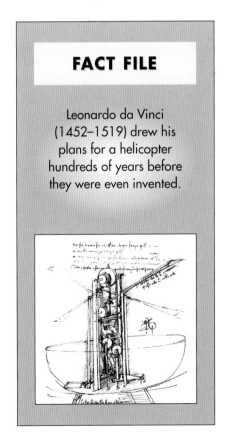

HOW ARE PLASTICS MADE?

When heated, plastics are a bit like modelling clay. It is this flexability that gives them their name. The word *plastic* means *capable of being molded* or *modeled*.

Molecules are the tiniest divisions of matter and act like the material from which they come. They are the basis for making plastic.

Chemists form certain molecules into long chains, as opposed to isolated, single molecules. In this process, new materials are produced. We call this *linkage polymerization*.

The material produced from the long-chain molecules are called *polymers*. They are the root of all plastics. In order to mold a polymer, it is ground into a powder or made into small pellets. Color is added, along with chemicals that give it more flexability. Plasticizers, which are chemicals that change rigid plastics into softer materials, are also used.

Whenever a plastic is manufactured, the molecules have to be rearranged in their long chains in a particlar way. To do this, chemicals have to be added.

The basic building blocks used in making plastics can vary greatly, from coal and salt to fibrous materials like wood and cotton.

A polymer of soft plastic

FACT FILE

Buttons are a good example of the different sizes, colors and shapes that can be produced from plastic.

WHY IS PLASTIC SO IMPORTANT?

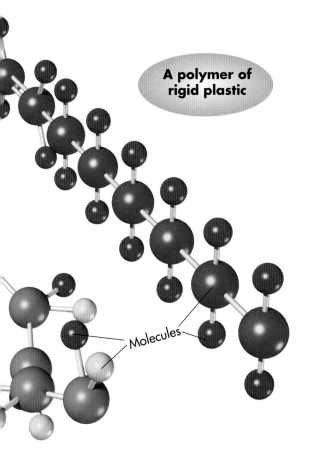

A polymer of rigid plastic

Molecules

FACT FILE

Plastic is a very versatile material. It can even be made flexible enough to make something like a raincoat.

Plastic is a popular material that has many uses. Probably not a day goes by in our lives when we do not use or touch a plastic product.

Plastics have many unique properties, which make them useful for special purposes. They resist the flow of electricity, they insulate against heat, they are light in weight, and they wear extremely well.

Plastic is such a good insulator that it is used to cover copper wires in everyday household wiring. Tools, such as screwdrivers, have plastic handles to provide insulation for the electrician, in case an electrical current is accidentally switched on.

Plastics made from organic compounds, such as ethene, can be incredibly strong. Racing car bodies are made from plastic that has been reinforced with glass fiber.

WHEN WAS CLAY FIRST USED?

A traditional potter's wheel

Clay is believed to have been used in the making of ceramic objects for at least 15,000 years. Fragments of clay pots have been found dating back to the Neolithic period, over 10,000 years ago.

As early as 5,000 years ago, people learned how to make their clay pots stronger and watertight by using fire. People soon discovered that by burning clay, its properties changed completely.

The uses of clay broadened from making small vessels to building materials. Clay-based bricks and tiles were among the first composite materials. Egyptian wall paintings of 5,000 years ago show clay workers making such bricks and pots.

The more adept people became at using clay, the more intricate the products were. Some pottery, which dates back thousands of years, shows a high artistic quality in its production. Examples of this are common from the Far East.

Through the ages, the use of clay in construction increased. Today, ceramics is still a huge industry worldwide.

FACT FILE

Ancient brick-makers fired bricks in *kilns* to produce building materials that were intended to last.

WHEN DID GOLD MINING BEGIN?

Although the time cannot be pinpointed exactly, it is widely believed that gold mining began about 5,000 years ago. The first gold was mined in Egypt. Egypt remained the center of gold production until the first century. Egyptian wall paintings show gold mining in its various stages of production. In those days, gold was mined from water. This was achieved by sifting out the lighter sands in the water to leave the heavier gold particles behind. By 3,000 B.C., gold rings were used as a form of payment. With the exception of coins, gold was used primarily for decorative purposes.

Around 2,000 B.C., mine shafts were built to obtain the gold found in ores deep in the ground. The Greeks and Romans became particularly adept at this endeavor.

Panning for gold

FACT FILE

Gold standard was a monetary system in which the standard unit of currency was a fixed quantity of gold. It was first put into operation in Great Britain in 1821.

WHEN WAS PAPER FIRST MADE?

The first paper was made about 2,000 years ago in China by a man called Ts'ai Lun. He took the stringy inner bark of the mulberry tree and pounded it in water until it became a mass of flattened threads. He then placed this pulpy solution onto a flat tray of fine bamboo strips.

Water drained through the bamboo, and the threads in the bamboo were left to dry. The result was a flat, fibrous material considered to be the very first paper. As with all new discoveries, improvements were gradually made. One of these was to brush starch over the paper to improve it.

FACT FILE

The Chinese were the first people who knew how to make silk. European traders would make the long journey to take silk back to Europe.

The secret of papermaking soon became worldwide knowledge as Chinese traders traveled to Russia and the Middle East. From there, the art of papermaking spread to Europe.

A revolutionary invention, paper began to be produced in large quantities. The first continuous papermaking machine was developed in France in 1798 by Louis Robert. At the beginning of the next century, the Fourdrinier brothers in London developed the idea even further.

WHEN WERE THE FIRST BOOKS MADE?

The Diamond Sutta, the oldest printed book known, was made in 868 A.D.

The first books were made about 4,000 years ago by the Egyptians. They took flattened layers of papyrus stems to make sheets of paper. The "books" they made were collections of rolled papyrus sheets and were very different from a book today.

In the middle of the fifth century, parchment, or sheep skin, replaced papyrus. Parchment sheets were placed on top of one another and bound down one side with leather tongs. But it wasn't until the Middle Ages that books as we know them today evolved. Vellum (calf skin) was made into sheets, and each piece was folded down the middle. Four vellum sheets made eight leaves and was considered a section. Unlike parchment, vellum was thick enough to be written on both sides. Finished sections were sewn together down the back fold (the spine) and covered with wooden boards front and back. The boards and spine were then covered with leather. The result was a book similar to that of today.

FACT FILE

In about 500 A.D., monks would spend endless hours on illuminated handwritten books. The work was slow and painstaking but worthwhile because it was another way to show their dedication to God.

WHERE WOULD YOU USE A BUNSEN BURNER?

Bunsen burners are used in scientific laboratories. They burn gas to heat materials. A bunsen burner is made up of a metal tube on a stand that is connected to a gas jet by a long rubber hose. The proportion of air that mixes with the gas is regulated by a number of adjustable openings at the lower end of the tube, which in turn determines the temperature of the flame. The flame produced is smokeless, a useful factor when working in a lab because the gas mixes with air before burning.

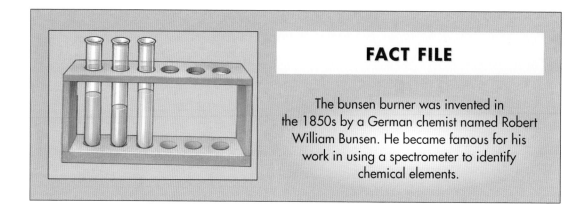

FACT FILE

The bunsen burner was invented in the 1850s by a German chemist named Robert William Bunsen. He became famous for his work in using a spectrometer to identify chemical elements.

WHERE WAS THE FIRST LOCK FOUND?

The oldest key-operated lock still in existence dates back to the late 700s B.C. It was found in the Assyrian capital of Khorsabad in the citadel of King Sargon II. Much older evidence of locks is apparent in Egyptian art from about 2000 B.C. These large locks were made of wood and had simple bolts with pegs that worked as pin-tumblers, a fitted key raising the tumblers and releasing the bolt.

Warded locks were first developed in Roman times. Warded locks operate with fixed ridges, or obstacles called *wards*, that prevent the wrong key from turning the lock. The notches cut into the correct key are designed to match the wards inside the lock, so that when it is turned the key connects past the wards, moving a spring inside the lock. This spring is attached to a bolt, or shackle, which slides to the locked or unlocked position when the spring moves. In a padlock, the bolt is the curved part that snaps into the body of the lock.

FACT FILE

With movable metal parts called *tumblers*, tumbler locks provide security against the wrong key opening a lock. Some type of tumbler arrangement is used in most door locks.

WHEN WAS FIRE DISCOVERED?

Human beings have been aware of fire since the most ancient of times. Evidence of this dates back thousands of years to charcoal and charred remnants of bone found in archeological digs.

It is likely, and logical, that early man was able to use fire before he knew how to actually create it. A tree struck by lightning and set afire, for instance, would provide fire as long as individuals could keep it going.

Similarly, cavemen of old might have noticed sparks created by the movement of loose stones. But it was probably a long time before they realized it was the friction of two stones rubbing together that caused the sparks. It goes without saying that the first fire man experienced was probably a creation of the natural world around him.

FACT FILE

In 1709, an ironmaster named Abraham Darby discovered that coal could be turned into coke by baking it. He was then able to make better-quality iron in his furnaces.

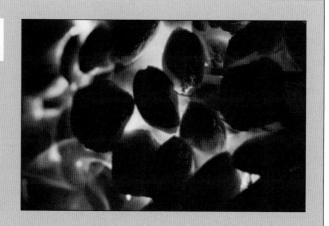

WHEN WERE MATCHES INVENTED?

The very first matches were designed by early human beings after they had discovered fire. Rubbing two pieces of flint together to create a spark is a basic fire-lighting creation.

The modern match, like those pictured above, was created after the discovery of a substance called *phosphorus*. It catches fire at low temperatures.

In the 19th century, a number of various matches were designed using phosphorus. Often, strips of wood were tipped with white or yellow phosphorous. However, white and yellow phosphorous is highly flammable and proved quite dangerous to use.

The first safety matches appeared with the introduction of nonpoisonous red phosphorous, introduced in Sweden in 1844. This phosphorous was painted on the surface of the match box rather than on the match-heads.

FACT FILE

Stone Age people made fire using a simple wooden stick called a *fire drill*. The drill was turned quickly over a piece of dry wood until it produced enough heat to start a fire.

WHEN WAS MORSE CODE DEVELOPED?

FACT FILE

Morse code was used a great deal during war because it was a quick and easy way of sending messages. Probably the most famous signal was *SOS*, which actually stood for "Save Our Souls."

S • • •

O – – –

S • • •

Morse code is a messaging system, which uses two kinds of signals, a short one called a *dot*, and a long one called a *dash*. The signals are sent via telegraphs. A transmitter sends a coded message in long and short bursts of radio waves along a wire. The receiver then translates the dots and dashes into their representative letters, numbers, and words.

Samuel Morse (1791-1872) was an American engineer who developed this system. He conceived the idea of some sort of communication via telegraph in 1832. After several years of work on the idea, Morse perfected it in 1838. However, at that time, telegraph lines did not exist across land, so there was no way Morse could put his code to use on a practical scale.

In 1843, the U.S. government allocated a sum of money to construct a telegraph line between Washington and Baltimore. Morse sent the first Morse code message along the line in 1844.

WHEN WAS BRAILLE INVENTED?

The Braille system was invented in 1829 by a blind gentleman named Louis Braille. He developed a system which would allow blind people to read and write. Today, it is one of the most widely used alphabets for the blind.

Braille is a system of dots. Each letter of the alphabet is represented by a combination of dots. These combinations are punched onto paper so that they appear as raised bumps. A blind person reads the dots by moving his or her fingers over the bumps, recognizing each letter to spell out the words.

There were earlier systems of reading for the blind. Back in the 16th century, alphabetic letters were carved into blocks of wood for the blind to read. This system was good for reading, but the blind could not see how to form the letters when they wanted to write.

The sensitive tip of the finger "feels" the Braille letters.

FACT FILE

Another means of communicating, by using flags, is called *semaphore*. Different flag positions represent different letters and numbers. This system was widely used between ships sailing near each other in the days before radio.

WHEN WERE FIREWORKS INVENTED?

Chinese crackers were probably the first fireworks made. This was around 2,000 years ago. They are still used in China and throughout the East to celebrate weddings, births, and religious festivals. They are also used to scare away evil spirits. It is probable that gunpowder was developed in China because they used potassium nitrate (saltpeter) to cure their meat, making it readily available.

For centuries, fireworks have been used in ancient Indian and Siamese ceremonies. The earliest recorded use of gunpowder in England was by the Franciscan monk Roger Bacon (born in 1214). He recorded his experiments with a mixture, which was very inadequate by today's standards, that was recognizable as gunpowder. His formula contained charcoal and sulphur because there was no natural source of potassium nitrate available.

FACT FILE

In January 1606, English Parliament established November 5 as a day of public thanksgiving. The day, known as Guy Fawkes Day, is still celebrated with bonfires, fireworks, and the carrying of "guys" through the streets.

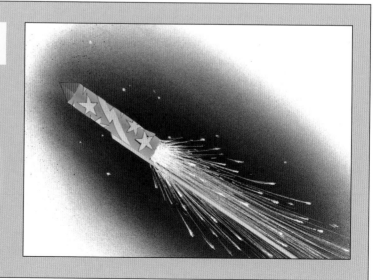

WHEN WAS GUNPOWDER FIRST USED?

The Chinese were the first to use gunpowder in warfare. By 1232, the Chinese had discovered black powder (gunpowder) and had learned to use it to make explosive bombs, as well as propelling forces for rockets. Later, drawings made in military documents show powder rockets tied to arrows and spears.

When the Mongols laid siege to the city of K'ai-feng, the capital of Honan province, the Chinese defenders used weapons that were described as arrows of flying fire.

In the same battle, it was reported that the defenders dropped a kind of bomb from the walls of the city described as "heaven-shaking thunder."

In the same century, rockets first appeared in Europe. Researchers believe the Mongols first used them in the Battle of Legnica in 1241. Reportedly, the Arabs used rockets in 1249.

FACT FILE

Guy Fawkes is best known for his efforts to blow up the Parliament building in 1605. This became known as the "Gunpowder Plot." His plan, however, failed, and he was arrested on November 4, 1605.

WHO SPLIT THE FIRST ATOM?

Ernest Rutherford (1871–1937) was a physicist who studied radioactivity. He found several different forms of radiation and also discovered that elements change as a result of radioactive decay. He received the Nobel Prize for his work. Rutherford went on to discover the nucleus of the atom, and in 1919, he split an atom for the first time.

Electron

Electron orbit

Neutron

Proton

Nucleus

He described the atom as a tiny, dense, positively charged core called a *nucleus*, in which nearly all the mass is concentrated. The light, negative constituents, called *electrons*, circulate around the core at some distance, much like planets revolve around the sun.

FACT FILE

Atoms become linked to other atoms by electrical bonds, which work like chemical hooks. Some atoms carry only one of these hooks, while others may have many.

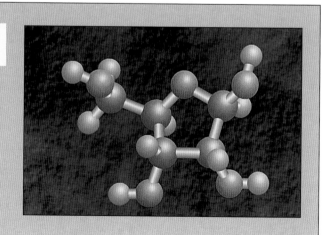

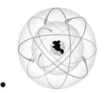

WHEN WAS ATOM STRUCTURE DISCOVERED?

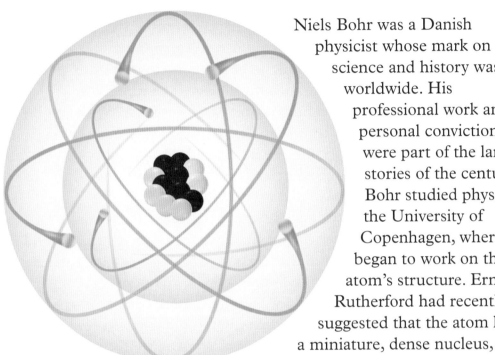

Niels Bohr was a Danish physicist whose mark on science and history was worldwide. His professional work and personal convictions were part of the larger stories of the century. Bohr studied physics at the University of Copenhagen, where he began to work on the atom's structure. Ernest Rutherford had recently suggested that the atom had a miniature, dense nucleus, surrounded by a cloud of nearly weightless electrons. There were a few problems with this model, however. Bohr proposed adding to the model, and this proved to be a huge leap forward in making theory fit the experimental evidence that other physicists had brought to light. A few inaccuracies remained to be solved by others over the next few years, but his essential idea was proved correct.

He received the Nobel Prize for his work in 1922, and it is what he is most famous for. He was only 37 years old at the time and went on to make many other discoveries.

FACT FILE

Niels Bohr helped to develop the atomic bomb in 1943.

WHERE DID THE IDEA OF THE LAVA LAMP COME FROM?

Edward Craven Walker was a Singapore native who flew reconnaissance missions for the Royal Air Force. One day, while visiting a pub in Hampshire, England, he became fascinated by an egg timer on a shelf behind the bar. The timer was essentially a blob of solid wax suspended in a clear liquid in a cocktail shaker. Once the shaker was dropped into the boiling water with an egg, the egg was done when the wax melted and floated to the top. As Walker looked at the egg timer, he envisioned what would become the lava lamp.

Walker sought the inventor of the egg timer and discovered that he had died without patenting it. He spent the better part of the next 15 years perfecting a way to mass-produce his "astro lamp." The theory behind his novelty lamp was relatively simple–enclose two liquids, which are similar in density and insoluble in one another, and apply heat. The most common insoluble liquids are oil and water. However, oil is nowhere near dense enough to achieve the desired result. What chemicals did Walker use? The recipe is a trade secret. Only the manufacturers of the lava lamps know the exact ingredients.

FACT FILE

This lamp was popular in the psychedelic 1960s. Soon, more than seven million lava lamps were being sold each year. Just as quickly, the fad ended.

WHY ARE MICROSCOPES USED?

The microscope enables us to see minute things, which are otherwise invisible to the naked eye. Its name comes from the Greek word *mikros* for "small" and *skopos* for "watcher." The instrument is indeed a "watcher of small things."

Objects under the microscope appear bigger when we bring them closer to the eye. When they get too close, anything less than 10 inches (25.5cm), they become blurred and are out of focus. But objects can be brought nearer and still stay in focus, with the aid of a simple convex lens, placed between the eye and the object.

Antonie van Leeuwenhoek (1632–1723) discovered ground glass lenses, which he used to examine the world about him. In the 1670s, he made his first crude microscope with a tiny lens. He was the first person to see microscopic life, such as bacteria, yeast, and living blood cells. From his pioneering work came the microscope–an instrument which is now used in every branch of science and industry.

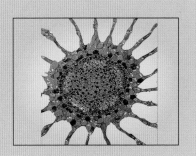

FACT FILE

Some microscopes are so powerful they can magnify the smallest objects. This plant cell would be invisible to the human eye without the use of magnification.

WHEN WERE CANALS BUILT?

A large commercial shipping canal

People have used canals to transport heavy goods for thousands of years. Researchers believe the first canals were built to join together existing rivers, making a transportation route. The city of Venice in Italy was built on a system of canals rather than roads. Much earlier, six thousand years ago, the Aztec city of Tenochitlan built an impressive system of canals in the city for transportation.

However, the most popular time of canal building was much more recent. The industrial revolution was responsible for the resumption of canal building. There was a major need during this era for cheap and easy methods to transport goods from factories to seaports. Horse-drawn canal boats and steam-powered canal boats were faster than carrying cargo by horse-drawn carts along the road.

FACT FILE

Locks are an essential feature of any canal. Some canals have no locks, such as the Gloucester and Sharpness Canal, although it does have a lock at either end.

WHEN WAS THE FIRST METAL BRIDGE BUILT?

The Industrial Revolution brought about the introduction of metal bridges. In the past, bridges were constructed of stone and timber, which were available in large quantities. Iron was used because it was much stronger than wood or stone and was usually less expensive to produce. The number of bridges made from timber or masonry declined.

The first-ever metal bridge was built in England in 1779. The Coalbrookdale Bridge, which spanned the River Severn, was designed by Thomas Pritchard and built by Andrew Darby. This bridge, the first to be built solely of iron, spanned almost 100 feet across the river in an almost perfect semicircular arrangement of cast-iron pieces.

FACT FILE

The drawbridge originated in medieval Europe to defend castles and towns. It was operated by a counterweight and winch. In the late 19th century, drawbridges began to be built specifically to aid navigation. The Tower Bridge in London is a good example.

THE MODERN
WORLD

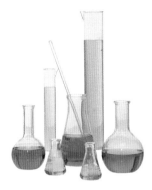

CONTENTS

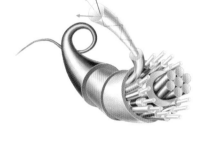

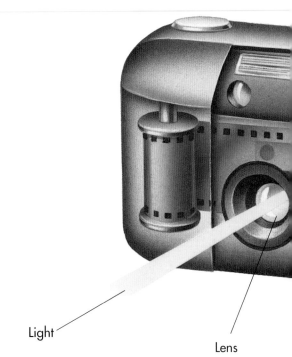

Light

Lens

FACT FILE

Insects' eyes are made up of hundreds of tiny lenses. The images from all these lenses are put together by the insect's brain. Like us, insects can see in color.

HOW DOES A CAMERA TAKE PICTURES?

The human eye is actually a type of camera. When you look around, your eyes actually "take pictures" of the things that you see. The lens in your eye acts just like the lens in a camera. The retina of your eye acts like the film in a camera. In a camera, light acts on a specially prepared surface of the film. If light didn't have any effect on certain chemically prepared substances, photography would be impossible.

When we open and close the shutter of a camera quickly, light comes in and strikes the film. When this happens, a chemical reaction takes place on the film. Certain tiny grains of silver bromide undergo a change. The film is taken out of the camera and treated with various chemicals to make the print visible and prevent further changes when exposed to light.

Digital cameras are a recent development. They convert the image they receive into electrical signals that are stored. These signals can then be read by a computer and used to produce a picture on the screen, which can be printed out.

How a camera works

Film

FACT FILE

Before photography, we could see only a mirror image of ourselves or have a portrait painted by an artist. Now, most people have a camera.

HOW IS CAMERA FILM MADE?

There are several steps in making camera film. First, gelatin is mixed with silver nitrate and potassium bromide to form a warm, gooey substance. This process requires total darkness as the silver crystals are sensitive to light. The nitrate and potassium, combined as potassium nitrate, are then washed away, leaving the silver bromide crystals in the gelatin in a liquid we call *emulsion*.

The actual film is made by treating cotton fibers or wood pulp with acetic acid, making a white flaky product called *cellulose acetate*. This is dissolved, and the mixture forms a clear, thick fluid, which is known as *dope*.

Feeding the dope evenly onto chromium-plated wheels, the wheels turn as the heat drives off the solvents. The dope becomes a thin, maleable, transparent sheet. Then, the film base is covered with the emulsion, with the dry film being cut into its designated widths and wound onto spools.

It is then ready to be placed into your camera. When you take a picture, light strikes the film and an image is formed.

HOW DOES A TELEPHONE WORK?

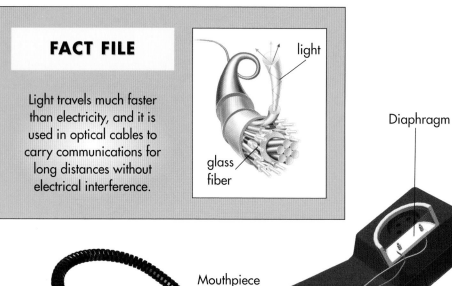

FACT FILE

Light travels much faster than electricity, and it is used in optical cables to carry communications for long distances without electrical interference.

light

glass fiber

Diaphragm

Mouthpiece

Earpiece

Wire

Telephones transmit speech messages along wires by means of electrical signals. They were invented in 1876. In the handset of a telephone is a loudspeaker and a very small microphone, which contains granules of carbon. When you talk into the microphone, the sound waves of your voice cause a metal diaphragm to vibrate, and this presses against the carbon granules. The vibrations vary depending on the sound. They change the very small amount of current flowing out along the wires to the receiver of another telephone.

When the electric current carrying the signal reaches the receiver handset, the same variations in the current run through an electro-magnet. This causes another diaphragm to vibrate in the earpiece, accurately reproducing the sound of the speaker's voice. Complex switching is needed to allow the call you make to reach the right person.

HOW DO RADIOS WORK?

Radio signals are transmitted using a carrier wave. Radio waves form part of the electromagnetic spectrum. Radio waves with the longest wavelengths are bounced off a layer high up in the earth's atmosphere, called the *ionosphere*. In this way, radio messages can be bounced for very long distances.

A radio transmitter changes, or modulates, a radio wave in order to convey information. In AM radio, the height of the carrier wave is altered according to the sound picked up by a microphone. In FM radio, the frequency, or distance between the peaks in the radio wave, is changed. The radio receiver picks up these signals, amplifies, and then decodes them. If the signal is weak, AM radio can sound crackly, which is why it is being replaced by FM radio, which gives much clearer reception.

FACT FILE

Radios are used for many different purposes. This firefighter, for example, will need his or her radio to be in constant communication with the main control as well as with other firefighters. Should he or she need assistance at any time, the radio should speed up any rescue.

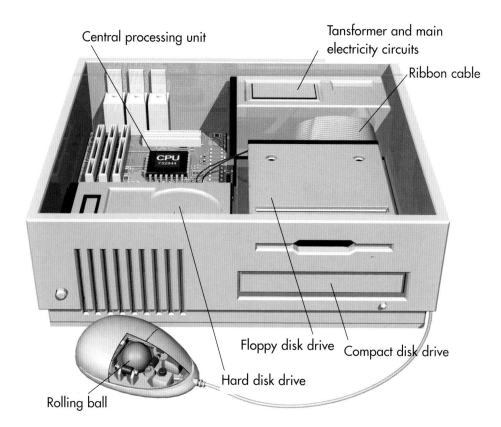

Central processing unit

Tansformer and main electricity circuits

Ribbon cable

Floppy disk drive

Compact disk drive

Hard disk drive

Rolling ball

HOW DO COMPUTERS WORK?

FACT FILE

Any modern electrical device needs a large number of connections to join together all the small components needed for it to work. Printed circuits are complex electrical circuits that are literally photographed on to a layer of insulating material. This makes them light, compact, and inexpensive.

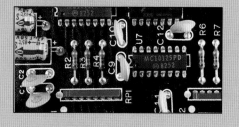

A computer is a piece of equipment that processes information rapidly and accurately. It processes words, pictures, sounds, and numbers. Some computers can make billions of calculations per second.

The heart of a computer is a microprocessor, which contains millions of tiny electronic devices on a silicon chip. Other chips form the computer's memory, where information is stored until it is needed. New data can be inputted from the keyboard or imported via a floppy disk drive, CD, or DVD drive, or for the Internet along a telephone line.

WHAT DO SCIENTISTS WEAR AT WORK?

Scientists study germs and bacteria that carry diseases. Because many of these could be extremely dangerous if touched or breathed in, it is essential for scientists to wear protective clothing, such as masks, gloves, and body and head protection.

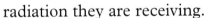

Scientists sometimes have to handle radioactive material. Exposure to radioactive radiation can be fatal to any living organism. For this reason, robots are used instead of human beings if at all possible.

When people do handle such substances, it is essential that they wear protective clothing and carry a meter that will record the exact level of radiation they are receiving.

FACT FILE

This symbol on a container or building warns that there is some radioactive material inside.

HOW IS NUCLEAR ENERGY PRODUCED?

Nuclear energy is produced by changes in the nucleus of an atom of a radioactive element, such as uranium or plutonium. This process is called *nuclear fission*.

A nucleus is split by bombarding the atom with a neutron particle. Each time the uranium atom is split in this way, it releases energy. It also produces three more neutrons, which then go on to split other uranium atoms. This is called a *chain reaction* because once started, it will continue the process of nuclear fission while releasing very large quantities of energy.

In a nuclear power station, this chain reaction has to be controlled. The reactor's core of uranium is surrounded with a substance that slows down and absorbs the escaping neutrons, causing the material to become hot. Steam generated by this heat is used to drive turbines to produce electricity.

FACT FILE

A nuclear power station produces electricity by using a nuclear reactor, which has a core of uranium, a highly radioactive material. Safety concerns have limited the use of these power stations.

HOW DO NUCLEAR WEAPONS WORK?

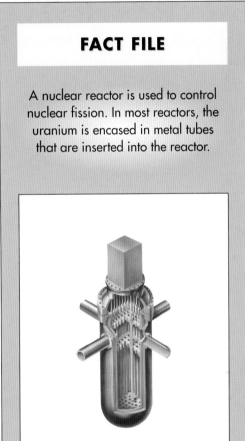

FACT FILE

A nuclear reactor is used to control nuclear fission. In most reactors, the uranium is encased in metal tubes that are inserted into the reactor.

An atom bomb is a form of uncontrolled nuclear fission. When a large enough mass of uranium is united, a fission reaction starts. The flood of neutrons emitted becomes so enormous that a vast amount of energy is released in a very short time, producing an atomic blast.

A hydrogen bomb has an atomic bomb at its core, but it is surrounded by a layer of light material. Using the power released from the fission of the uranium or plutonium core, this layer of material causes a fusion reaction like the one in the center of the sun. This nuclear fusion releases more heat energy than a fission explosion, as well as large amounts of radioactivity.

HOW DOES AN ELECTRIC MOTOR WORK?

Most powered devices located in the home contain an electric motor, which turns electric energy into movement. When an electric current passes along a wire in the field of a magnet, it exerts a force to move the wire. Usually, the magnet is still, while the coil carrying the current spins round inside it. Domestic motors run on alternating current, meaning the current in the coil is rapidly reversed so that the magnet's poles change direction, forcing the coil to make another half-turn. This process is repeated very rapidly as the motor turns.

When a motor runs from a direct current, which flows in only one direction, a device called a *commutator* reverses the current and causes the coil to rotate.

It is this motion that can be used to drive a large number of machines, such as washing machines, hairdriers, and food processors.

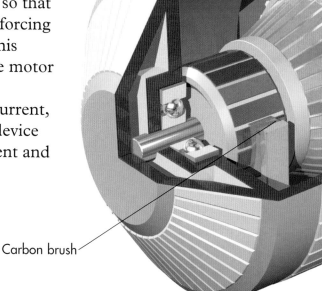

Carbon brush

FACT FILE

A voltmeter measures voltage. An electrical current flows from an area with high to low electrical potential, as in one battery terminal to another. The difference between the two is then measured in volts (V).

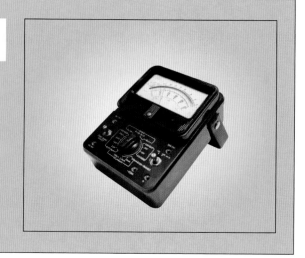

HOW ARE VEHICLES POWERED BY ELECTRICITY?

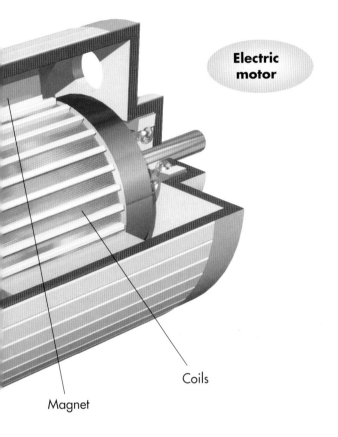

Electric motor

Magnet

Coils

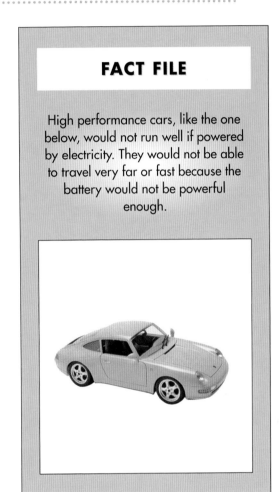

Electrically powered vehicles have been in use for many years. Powering cars with electricity presents certain problems, however, because the batteries are heavy and a car's energy requirement is high. This means that the distance an electric car can travel before it is recharged may be too low to be practical.

Where vehicles can obtain electrical energy from a fixed wire or track, there is no problem with electrical supply. Electrically powered trains, such as the ones used in France, are the fastest in the world.

Specially designed electrically powered wheelchairs and other vehicles enable disabled people to move about at the same speed as a pedestrian. These are powered by rechargeable batteries.

WHAT IS A TRANSISTOR?

Transistors are tiny devices that are found in computers, radios, television sets, and most other forms of electronic equipment. Larger models are sometimes used in industrial appliances. A transistor's

function is to control the flow of electric current by switching it on and off and to, where necessary, strengthen or amplify it. Until the 1950s, the most usual method of doing this was to use vacuum tubes. These were large, unreliable, and expensive both to produce and use. Early uses of transistors were to miniaturize personal calculators and to develop digital watches. During the following half-century, smaller and smaller transistors were developed, and today's modern computer chip may contain millions of them.

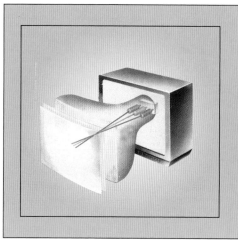

FACT FILE

The ability to amplify signals makes a transistor an essential part of radios and television sets. The broadcast waves that travel through the air generate weak currents in a radio or TV antenna. Transistors amplify these signals to produce sounds and pictures.

WHAT ARE PYLONS?

FACT FILE

In an electric lightbulb, an electrical current is passed through a very thin filament of metal. The filament becomes white hot and gives us light.

Electricity is used as a way of moving energy from place to place. It can take energy from burning coal in a power station into your home. Electricity is required for many things in our homes and at work. So, we need a way of getting the energy to travel. Giant masts called *pylons* have been erected all over the country. They are connected by powerful electrical cables. Energy travels down these cables at about 155,000 miles a second, which is nearly as fast as the speed of light.

WHEN IS A BAROMETER USED?

A barometer is used to measure changes in air pressure. Air pressure varies across different parts of the earth's surface, and these differences cause winds. Air moves from an area of high pressure, called an *anticyclone*, to an area of low pressure, called a *depression*. Depressions are usually associated with worsening weather conditions and rain. In a mercury barometer, the air pressure pushes down on the mercury, which is forced up the barometer to give an accurate reading. Air pressure is greatest at sea level, where it amounts to 14.7 lbs. per square inch. It is greatest there because that is the bottom of the atmosphere. At higher altitudes, the pressure is less.

FACT FILE

The higher we go, the less air pressure there is. This is why space suits and the cabins of high-flying planes are pressurized. They are designed to maintain the air pressure our bodies must have.

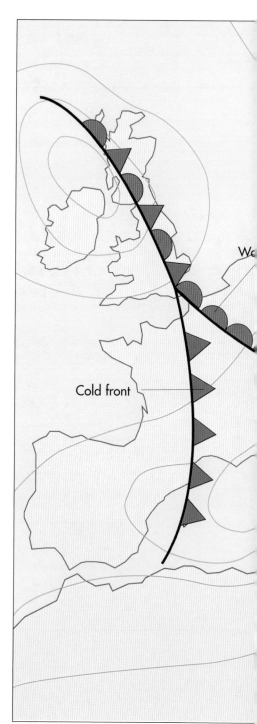

Cold front

WHEN DID WEATHER FORECASTING BEGIN?

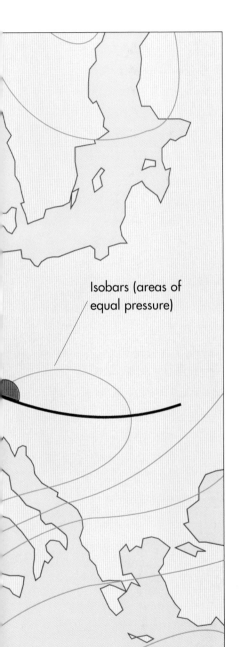

Isobars (areas of equal pressure)

People have been able to forecast the weather for hundreds of years. Meteorologists have used simple instruments like thermometers, rain gauges, barometers, and wind gauges for many years, but with the advent of satellite photography, weather forecasting has been improved. Now that computers are used, more accurate forecasting is possible.

Traditional forecasters have been known to use pine cones, which open and close according to the humidity in the air. An open cone means dry weather. Seaweed also responds to changes in humidity. Dry seaweed indicates dry weather.

FACT FILE

There is an old saying regarding the weather:
If the oak tree has its leaves before the ash tree, then it will be a nice summer.

WHY ARE OPTICAL FIBERS USEFUL?

An optical fiber is made of fine strands of glass, along which pulses of light can travel. Light travels much faster than electricity so optical cables are used to carry communications for long distances without electrical interference. The light travels along tiny glass fibers, usually packed into large bundles capable of carrying many thousands of messages at the same time.

FACT FILE

Most communication today is carried by satellite. Radio, telephone, and television messages are transmitted around the world with incredible speed. These satellites orbit the earth so that they appear to be in the same place all the time—even though the earth continues to spin around. This is possible because a satellite's orbit speed matches the earth's rotational speed. These are known as *geo-stationary* orbits.

When you talk on the telephone, your voice is turned into laser light signals and sent down very thin fiber glass tubes called *optical fibers*. Up to 150,000 different conversations can be sent down just *one* of these optical fibers.

Optical fiber is also used for decorative lighting. Light is reflected down thousands of tiny glass fibers seen on some artificial Christmas trees.

WHY DOES COMMUNICATION CONTINUE TO IMPROVE?

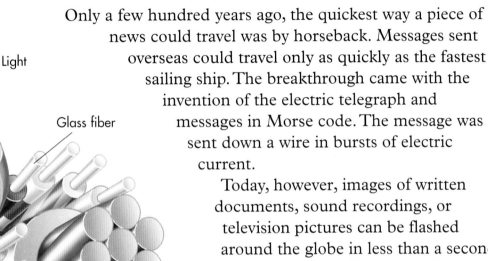

Light

Glass fiber

Only a few hundred years ago, the quickest way a piece of news could travel was by horseback. Messages sent overseas could travel only as quickly as the fastest sailing ship. The breakthrough came with the invention of the electric telegraph and messages in Morse code. The message was sent down a wire in bursts of electric current.

Today, however, images of written documents, sound recordings, or television pictures can be flashed around the globe in less than a second by satellite and radio communications. Several satellites, in different orbits, are required to give coverage over the whole world. Different satellites are used to reflect signals for different media, such as telephone messages and television pictures.

FACT FILE

Mobile phones work by using low-powered microwaves to send and receive messages to and from a base station. Otherwise known as a *cellular phone*, a mobile allows calls to be received and made wherever the caller happens to be.

WHY ARE WIND TURBINES USED AS A POWER SOURCE?

When oil, gas, and coal run out, people will need other sources of energy to fuel their cars and light their houses. Concerns about pollution resulting from electrical power production have led to the development of wind turbines. Large windmills can be found on exposed and windy areas in certain parts of the country.

Strong, steady winds turn the windmill blades. As the blades spin, they turn a shaft that generates electricity. These modern wind turbines come in several shapes. Large groups of them are called *wind farms*. The windmills of a wind farm can power generators to produce electricity for hundreds of homes.

FACT FILE

The principle of the windmill has been known since ancient times, but little is known about its use before the 12th century. Windmills are still used today to pump water for livestock, household use, or for irrigation.

WHY ARE SOLAR PANELS ATTACHED TO ROOFTOPS?

We are aleways looking for new sources of energy. The sun produces vast amounts of energy, but only a small portion of it reaches the earth. If we could use just a small part of this energy, it would fulfill all the world's potential need for power. One way of harnessing the sun's power is by using solar panels. Today, many homes generate some of their own power. Solar panels attached to rooftops absorb the sun's energy, which is later used to heat domestic water supplies. The first solar power station was built in 1969 at Odeillo, in France. It uses solar power to generate energy, and has many solar panels to collect as much energy from the sun as possible. Some day, scientists hope to collect sunlight in space and beam it back to the earth.

FACT FILE

The sun's rays heat water in a pipe system within the solar panels. Cold water enters the pipes and flows through the panel, heating up as it goes. Hot water is collected from the pipes and stored for future use.

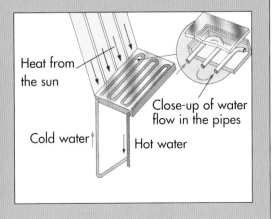

Heat from the sun

Close-up of water flow in the pipes

Cold water

Hot water

WHEN WAS TELEVISION INVENTED?

An early broadcast

Televison was not "invented" by a particular person but evolved over a period of time. The first system was made in the United States by G.R. Carey in 1875, by focusing an object through a lens onto a bank of photoelectric cells. The individual cells regulated the electricity that would be passed on to a light bulb, and a crude outline of the object would appear in lights.

In 1923, the first real pictures were sent over wires. There was also a great improvement in television camera technology.

By 1945, television as we know it today, had been developed.

Technological developments continue to improve the quality of television pictures today.

FACT FILE

By using communication satellites, TV programs can be beamed to the most remote parts of the world, including the Amazon jungle!

WHEN DID THE INTERNET BEGIN?

The Internet was created in 1983. The concept of the Internet originated from the U.S. Defense department, that had a basic version of the Internet set up as a secure system for their information.

The Internet originated from basically an academic origin, as a framework connecting numerous computer networks together. It has rapidly developed into a very popular commercial medium. By the mid-1990s, millions of computers around the world were connected to the "World Wide Web."

Technology is always changing. The Internet truly exemplifies the capabilities of modern developments.

FACT FILE

Modern communications have affected our lives in many ways. Since the 1980s, the mobile phone has proved to be an increasingly popular means of communication. It was publicly introduced in Chicago in 1983, and was a success from the beginning.

WHEN WAS THE CN TOWER BUILT?

The CN Tower in Toronto, Canada, is a communications and observation tower. This building was completed in 1976, and at that time was the world's tallest free-standing structure.

The 20th century saw an explosion in communications technology. The first radio broadcast was made early in the century, when Reginald A. Fessenden transmitted music and words in 1906. By the 1920s, radio provided a major form of entertainment for people worldwide. In 1926, a Scottish engineer named John Logie Baird developed the first successful television set.

FACT FILE

Communication satellites are used to carry communications such as radio, television, and telephone messages around the world. These satellites are "parked" in an orbit where they remain in position over the same part of the earth's surface.

WHAT IS A MODEM USED FOR?

A personal computer

Computers that are connected to a telephone line use a device called a *modem*. It turns signals into a form that can be transmitted along a telephone line. The name *modem* comes from the term "Modulator-Demodulator." This device modulates, or changes, the digital signal from a computer into an analog signal, which is the type of signal that travels along telephone lines. The modem decodes, or demodulates, the signals it receives back so they can be read by the computer. Some modems are "voiceband"; that means they enable digital terminal equipment to communicate over telephone channels, which are designed around the narrow bandwidth requirements of the human voice.

FACT FILE

Robots are machines that "think" with a computer brain which tells them what to do. A factory robot is often just a moving arm.

WHERE WOULD A CATALYTIC CONVERTER BE USED?

An automobile's internal combustion engines gives off various harmful chemicals, including carbon monoxide. The catalyctic converter has been designed to reduce these exhaust emissions. A substance called a *catalyst*–in most converters this is a blend of the metals platinum, palladium, and rhodiumin–causes these pollutants to change into safer materials.

The catalytic converter is installed in an automobile's exhaust system. As the exhaust gases pass through the converter, the catalyst causes carbon monoxide and the other pollutants to change to oxygen, nitrogen, water, and carbon dioxide.

FACT FILE

Cars with catalytic converters have to use fuel that contains no lead or phosphorus. Both of these substances coat the catalyst's surface, making it ineffective.

WHEN DID THE CANNING OF FOOD AND DRINK BEGIN?

For centuries, people have tried to find better ways to preserve food. Peter Durand, of England, was granted the first patent for a "tin

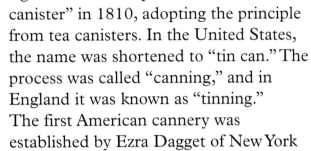

canister" in 1810, adopting the principle from tea canisters. In the United States, the name was shortened to "tin can." The process was called "canning," and in England it was known as "tinning." The first American cannery was established by Ezra Dagget of New York City in 1819 for preserving fish. Soon, other foodstuffs including fruit, vegetables, and meat were being "canned" (sometimes in glass jars) all over the United States and the world. Food being preserved in this way must be heated enough to kill bacteria that causes it to spoil. The tin can or glass container must be air-tight when sealed.

FACT FILE

In 1810, a French chef named Nicholas Appert discovered a way of preserving food by packing food into wide-mouth bottles. He sealed the bottles and then lowered them into a boiler filled with hot water. A lid was added so that the bottles would heat in boiling water. Some foods, like fruit and vegetables, may also be preserved by pickling, then stored in jars.

WHERE ARE THERMOPLASTICS USED?

There are two basic types of plastics, thermsetting plastics and thermoplastics. The difference is how they react when heated. Thermoplastics can be melted over and over again.

Their polymer chains do not form into cross-links so the chains can move freely when heated. Because they are so flexible to handle and require as few as ten seconds to set, thermoplastics are widely used. Thermoplastics can be dispersed in liquid to produce durable high-gloss paints and lacquers. Some thermoplastics tend to lose their shape when exposed to constant pressure over a long period of time. Polytetrafluoroethylene is a thermoplastic which resists heat and chemicals and slides easily. It is used for cable insulation, bearings, valve seats, gaskets, frying pan coatings, slides, and cams.

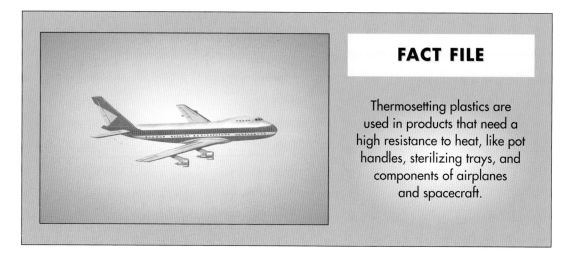

FACT FILE

Thermosetting plastics are used in products that need a high resistance to heat, like pot handles, sterilizing trays, and components of airplanes and spacecraft.

WHERE DO RECYCLED GOODS COME FROM?

Recycled goods come from everyday waste, including cans, glass containers, newspapers, and office paper. Instead of throwing away this waste, recycling ensures that we reuse materials by collecting, processing, and remanufacturing them. There are also recycling programs that collect our old magazines, plastic goods, and even unused motor oil.

The process of recycling is useful to both the economy and the environment. It helps save raw materials and energy that would otherwise be used to make new products. It decreases the amount of material in landfill sites where waste is deposited, and it helps reduce the pollution that often accompanies trash disposal.

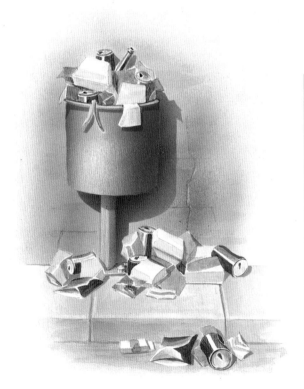

FACT FILE

When you buy a new car, it may not be quite as new as you think. Up to 40 percent of the steel may have come from old cars. Recycling scrap steel saves raw materials and energy.

THE SOLAR

SYSTEM

CONTENTS

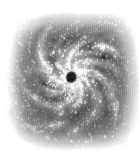

WHAT IS THE MOON?

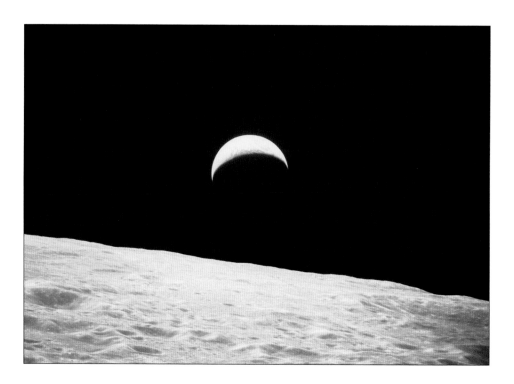

The moon is the earth's only satellite. It has been orbiting our planet for at least 4,000 million years. It is a rocky sphere about 2,155 mi. (3,476 km) across, which is about one-quarter the size of the earth.

Scientists believe that the moon formed when another planet about the size of Mars collided with the earth. The collision caused a large mass of molten (liquid) rock to splash into space. This molten rock quickly formed into a sphere, and the moon cooled into its solid form. The moon's surface is heavily pitted by collisions with debris, such as asteroids.

FACT FILE

Living things need air and water to live, and neither of these is available on the moon. The moon also has extreme temperature variances between the lunar day and night.

WHAT IS THE MOON MADE OF?

The moon is a rocky satellite, made of similar material to earth's. It has an outer layer, or mantle, of rock and a core that is probably composed mostly of iron. Unlike the earth's liquid mantle, the interior of the moon is cool and solid. There is little or no volcanic activity on the moon.

However, while it was cooling, floods and streams of lava ran across the moon's surface. The moon also has mountain ranges, many of which are the remains of impact craters and volcanoes that were active when the moon was still hot. There are some large valleys called *rilles*, which can be hundreds of miles in length and look a little like riverbeds.

FACT FILE

The first man on the moon was Neil Armstrong, accompanied by Buzz Aldrin, on July 20, 1969. They traveled to the moon on a spaceship called Apollo 11.

WHAT IS THE EARTH MADE OF?

The big ball that we call the earth is mostly made from rock. On the outside, there is a layer of hard rock, while inside the rock is melted. Less than one-third of the earth's surface is land, while more than two-thirds of the surface is water.

The outer layer of rock, which we often call the earth's *crust*, is between 10 to 30 miles thick. The continents of land are formed by the higher parts of this crust, and the seas, oceans, and

FACT FILE

The earth is thought to be about 4,600 million years old. The oldest rocks discovered are about 3,800 years old. We can calculate the age of the earth by examining meteorites and changes in atomic structure.

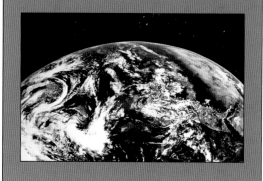

larger lakes by the lower. The actual crust is divided into two layers. The upper layer is made of granite. Under the layer of granite lies a thick layer of very hard rock, called *basalt*.

Scientists believe that at the central core of the earth is an enormous ball of molten iron, more than 4,000 miles in diameter.

HOW MUCH DOES THE ATMOSPHERE WEIGH?

The earth is surrounded by a thick blanket of air called the *atmosphere*. It is made up of about 20 different gases, the two most important being oxygen and nitrogen. It also contains particles of water and dust.

Air is a form of matter, so like all matter, it has weight. Weight is the measure of the pull of gravity on matter. That means that a two-pound bag of sugar being pulled with a force of two pounds. In the same way, each particle of dust and gas in the atmosphere is "pulled" earthwards. As a kind of vast ocean of air, the atmosphere weighs quite a bit–about 5,700 quadrillion (5,700,000,000,000,000) tons! The earth's atmosphere is one of the crucial factors that allows it to support life.

FACT FILE

Our knowledge of air pressure has enabled us to understand the physics of flight. Air passing over the top of a plane's wings reduces in pressure, allowing higher pressure under the wings to exert an upward force, so the airplane can fly.

WHY DOES THE EARTH TRAVEL AROUND THE SUN?

According to one theory about the origin of our solar system is that a huge dust cloud was formed about 5 billion years ago. Spinning through space, it gradually flattened into a disk, and the hot center formed the sun. At the same time, the outer portions of the dust cloud spun off into space, breaking away from the center in swirling masses to become the planets. The reason these planets, including the earth, didn't fly off into space was due to the gravitational pull of the sun.

It is this gravitational force that keeps the earth revolving around the sun in what we call its *orbit*. The speed a planet moves in its orbit depends on its distance from the sun. When it is closer, it moves faster. The earth moves at 18.8 miles per second when closest to the sun and 18.2 miles per second at its furthest point.

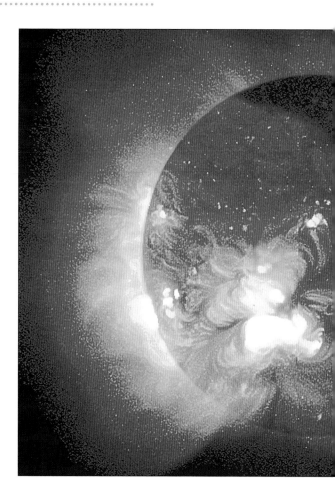

FACT FILE

Other planets that revolve around the sun include Mercury and Pluto. Mercury is the closest planet to the sun and moves at an average speed of 29.8 miles per second.

WHAT IS THE SUN MADE OF?

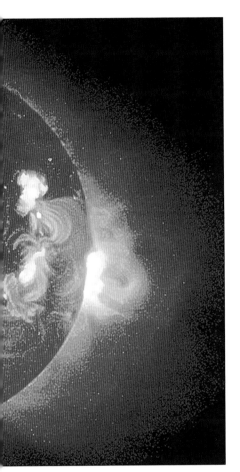

The sun is a great ball of hot gases, made up of many layers. Astronomers have obtained what they know about the sun by using special instruments. These instruments allow scientists to find out what these glowing gases are and what they are made up of. It also allows them to take photographs of the sun's corona without damaging their eyes. Finally, these instruments study radio waves that are emitted by the sun. Because the earth's atmosphere stops many of the sun's radiations from reaching earth, scientists send instruments high up into the atmosphere. These space probes help them learn more about the sun.

FACT FILE

Without the sun, life on earth would be impossible. The atmosphere would be frozen, no green plants would be living, and there would be no rain.

WHAT IS THE MILKY WAY?

One of the most spectacular features of the night sky is the Milky Way, which stretches from one horizon to the other. The Milky Way is the name of our galaxy.

If it could be looked down on from above, our galaxy would appear as a huge disk, round and flat like an enormous watch. But from our vantage point, we look out towards its edge. From this edge we see, curving around us, millions of stars belonging to the Milky Way.

FACT FILE

Containing at least 3,000,000,000 stars, this galaxy is so big we can hardly imagine its size. While the light from the sun takes eight minutes to reach earth, the light from the middle of the galaxy takes about 27,000 years to reach the sun.

WHAT IS A STAR?

Stars are huge balls of burning gas that are scattered throughout the universe. They burn for millions of years, giving off both light and heat. Stars produce energy by a process called *nuclear fusion*. The coolest stars are red and dim, while the hottest stars give off blue-white light. The temperatures on their surface range from 6,330°F (3,500°C) for cooler stars to over 72,030°F (40,000°C) for the hottest stars.

A new star is born when gas and dust are drawn together by gravity, forming a large clump. It heats up until nuclear fusion begins, when the new star appears in the sky.

FACT FILE

Stars die when they use up all their fuel and burn out, but this process takes many millions of years. Towards the end of its life, a star starts to run out of hydrogen to power its nuclear fusion. It starts to cool, becoming a red giant.

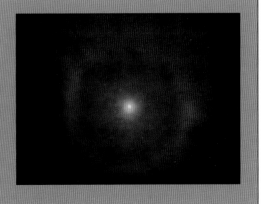

WHY DO STARS APPEAR TO SHINE?

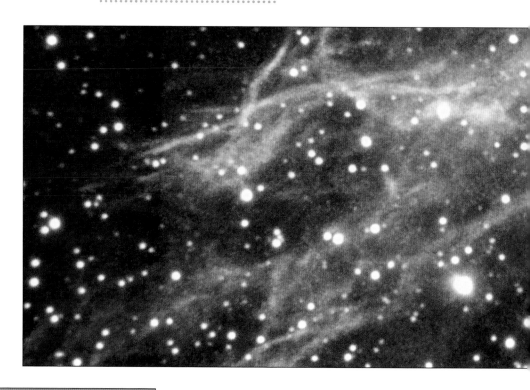

FACT FILE

The farthest stars in our galaxy are 80,000 light-years away. The nearest star to the earth is our own sun, which is 94 million mi. (152 million km) away.

Just like the sun, a star is a ball of hot gas that shines with its own light. One of the things we notice when we look at the stars in the night sky is that they appear to twinkle. This "twinkling" effect is caused by various, unsteady substances in the atmosphere between the earth and space, bending the light from the star.

Scientists believe that hydrogen atoms in the very core of stars burn to form helium. When this happens, it sets forth free energy, which flows steadily to its surface. Stars should be able to keep radiating this energy for millions of years.

WHEN DO YOU SEE A SHOOTING STAR?

Shooting stars, or meteors, are streaks of light that cross the night sky, although they can be seen for only one or two seconds. Meteors are caused when a solid piece of rock called a *meteoroid* plunges through the earth's atmosphere, burning up due to air friction. If a small fragment reaches the earth, which rarely happens, it is called a *meteorite*. Sometimes, these fragments of rock move through space as a meteor swarm, or stream. They move in regular paths through space. The larger fragments become detached and travel through space by themselves.

FACT FILE

This impact crater in Arizona was caused by a huge meteorite. The amount of energy this impact released would have been equivalent to hundreds of nuclear weapons.

WHAT IS A SUPERNOVA?

Sometimes, a star appears in the sky quite suddenly. This occurs when a pair of stars rotate together. These are called *binaries*. Usually there is one large star called a *red giant*, orbiting with a smaller, hotter star. The nova takes place when gas is drawn from the red giant into the smaller star, where the heat causes a massive explosion and emits large amounts of light. A supernova takes place when a star collapses as it begins to burn out. Suddenly it explodes, producing a huge amount of light energy. It leaves behind a tiny core of neutrons, which is the heaviest substance in the universe.

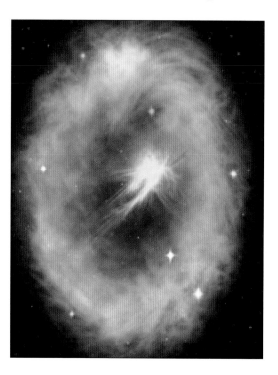

FACT FILE

Even with today's most powerful and advanced equipment, there is no visible limit to the universe.

WHAT IS A NEBULA?

FACT FILE

The only diffuse nebula visible to the naked eye is the beautiful Orion Nebula.

A nebula is a huge cloud of white-hot gas and solid material that whirls about in interstellar space, getting smaller and hotter all the time. As the gas cloud grows smaller, it throws off rings of gas. Each of these rings condenses to become a star. Based on appearance, nebulae can be divided into two broad classes: dark nebulae and bright nebulae. Dark nebulae appear as irregularly shaped black patches in the sky and blot out the light of the stars lying beyond them. Bright nebulae appear as faintly luminous, glowing surfaces. They either emit their own light or reflect the light of nearby stars.

WHAT ARE THE PLANETS OF THE SOLAR SYSTEM?

The four planets that are closest to the sun are called the inner planets. In order from the sun, they are Mercury, Venus, Earth, and Mars. The inner planets are different from the outer planets, which are farther away from the sun, because they are made of rock. Each of the inner planets has an atmosphere. However, except for earth, the atmospheres of the inner planets are very thin and poisonous to human beings. The outer planets, Jupiter, Saturn, Uranus, Neptune, and Pluto, are composed mostly of frozen gases. So although they are very large, they are comparatively light.

FACT FILE

Science fiction writers thought that life might exist beneath the thick clouds of Venus. We now know that conditions there are too extreme for life as we know it.

WHAT ARE THE RINGS OF SATURN?

FACT FILE

Pluto is the smallest and most remote planet on the edge of deep space. It was discovered in 1930 as a result of calculations to find out why Neptune's orbit was so irregular.

Shining rings of billions of tiny chips of ice, rock, and dust surround Saturn. The rings reflect light strongly and can be clearly seen through a telescope from the earth. Scientists first thought that Saturn had three wide rings, but we now know that the rings are actually composed of thousands of narrow ringlets. The rings are only 330 ft. (100 meters) thick, but extend into space for 50,000 mi. (76,000 km) The material in the rings was probably pulled by Saturn's gravity when the solar system was forming, or it might be the remains of a moon that has broken up. Recently, research from space probes has determined that some of the rings are braided, or twisted.

WHY IS NEPTUNE BLUE?

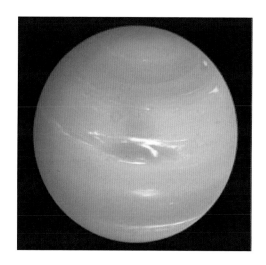

Neptune is covered with a blue ocean of liquid methane. It is a very cold place. At the farthest part of its orbit, it is 2,450 million mi. (4,000 million km) from the sun. Its surface temperature drops to −346°F (−210°C). Neptune is made of hydrogen, helium, and methane, and probably has a rocky core. It takes a remarkable 164.8 years to travel just once around the sun. Neptune was first identified in 1846, when astronomers found that an unidentified planet was disturbing the orbit of Uranus. Neptune has great storms, and one of these, the Great Dark Spot, was larger than the earth.

FACT FILE

Mars is covered with a stony desert that contains a great deal of iron oxide, making it appear rusty-red. Mars has small polar ice caps that grow larger during the Martian winter.

WHAT DOES VENUS LOOK LIKE?

Venus is often referred to as Earth's sister. The planet is a similar size to our own but there the resemblance ends. The temperature on the surface of the planet is nearly 930°F (500°C). The air is dense enough to crush a human in seconds, and the atmosphere consists partly of acid. The dark patches that you see on the surface of Venus are a layer of cloud 19 miles (30 km) thick. If we look past the clouds, we can see that Venus is a planet once ruled by volcanoes.

FACT FILE

Because Venus was the Roman goddess of love, astronomers have named many of the planet's features after famous women.

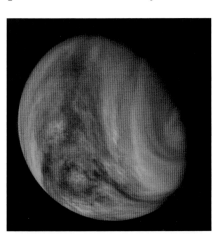

Scientists believe that there are at least 160 volcanoes that are larger than 62 miles (100 km) in diameter and more than 50,000 smaller ones. However, there is no evidence to indicate that these volcanoes are still active today.

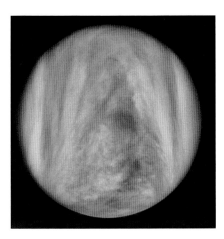

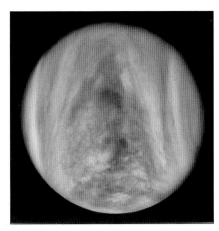

WHAT DOES THE EARTH LOOK LIKE FROM SPACE?

Salt Lake City, Utah

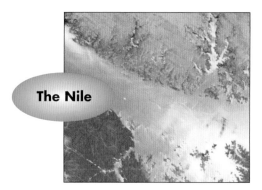

The Nile

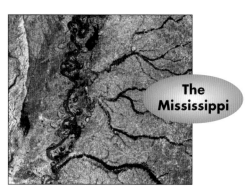

The Mississippi

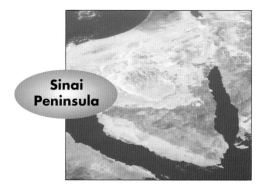

Sinai Peninsula

Earth is the third planet outward from the sun. Its single most outstanding feature is that its environment is the only place in the universe known to maintain life. Those who have gone into space have come back with a changed perspective and reverence for the planet Earth. The effect from space is obvious. One astronaut said after his trip, "My first view–a panorama of brilliant deep-blue ocean, shot with shades of green and gray and white–was of atolls and clouds."

FACT FILE

Pioneer 10 was the first human-made object to leave the solar system. It carried messages about life on Earth to be read by any extraterrestrial travelers who might meet the probe.

WHERE WOULD YOU SEE BAILY'S BEADS?

A total eclipse of the sun can be quite frightening, turning day into night in a spectacular fashion. However, as the moon appears to "eat" the sun, some incredibly beautiful special effects take place. Just before the sun disappears, a brilliant bright spot can be seen on the edge of the moon, a little like a diamond on a ring. This is caused by the last fingers of the sun's light filtering through valleys and mountain ranges on the moon. Sometimes, the bright spot can appear as an arc of glowing pearls, an effect known

as *Baily's Beads*, named after the British astronomer Francis Baily.

FACT FILE

It is important never to look directly at the sun, even during an eclipse. This can cause blindness.

WHY DO COMETS HAVE TAILS?

You cannot see the nucleus of a comet with the naked eye, but you can sometimes see its tail. It appears as a smear of light that moves very gradually across the sky. As a comet moves closer to the sun, the ice and other frozen gases in its nucleus begin to boil off, producing a long tail of gas and dust. The tail always points away from the sun because light and other forms of radiation from the sun push against the minute particles present within the tail.

Comets' tails differ in shape and size. Some are short and stubby, while others are long and slender. As the tail grows, the comet gains in speed as it nears the sun.

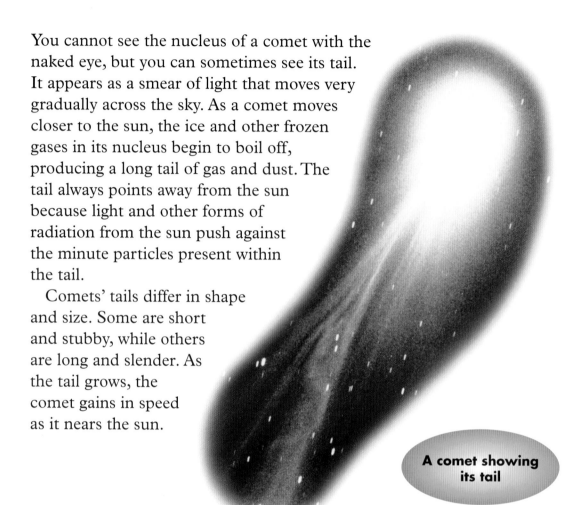

A comet showing its tail

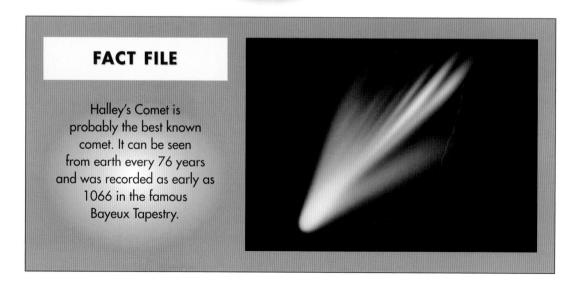

FACT FILE

Halley's Comet is probably the best known comet. It can be seen from earth every 76 years and was recorded as early as 1066 in the famous Bayeux Tapestry.

WHAT IS A BLACK HOLE?

Black holes are the "monsters" of the universe. Formed from the brightest of all explosions, supernovae, they soon become the darkest objects in space, emitting no light at all. A black hole is an area in space

where the force of gravity is so strong that even light cannot escape from it. Black holes are created when a burned-out star collapses. Eventually, it shrinks into a tiny sphere of material. The gravity of this material is so powerful that it pulls in everything around it. Even light itself is sucked into the black hole. Nothing that goes into a black hole ever comes out. We cannot see black holes, but we can sometimes identify them from the radio waves given off when a star is drawn into a black hole.

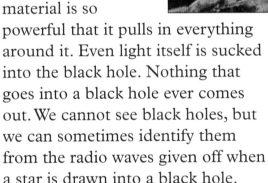

FACT FILE

Imagine space as a stretched-out sheet. If an object is placed on this sheet, it will create a dip, towards which other objects will be drawn if they come too close. A black hole creates such a steep dip that objects that enter it can never escape.

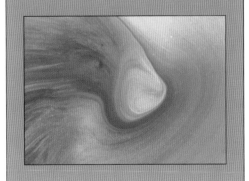

WHAT WAS THE BIG BANG?

Nobody knows how the universe began, but the most common theory is the Big Bang. According to this theory, the universe was formed from an immense explosion 13 billion years ago. Before the Big Bang, everything in the universe was packed into a tiny area, smaller than the nucleus of an atom. This point was called a *singularity* and was incredibly hot. It was released in an explosion so powerful that all of the matter in the singularity was blasted into an area larger than a galaxy in less than a fraction of a second. There is strong evidence to support this theory. The strongest "proof" is a weak signal that has been detected in space. This is thought to be an echo from the energy released by the force of the Big Bang.

FACT FILE

According to ancient Egyptian mythology, the fundamentals of life—air (Shu) and moisture (Tefnut)—came from the spittle of their sun god, Re. From the union of Shu and Tefnut came Geb, the earth god, and Nut, the sky goddess. The first human beings were born from Re's tears.

WHAT IS THE UNIVERSE MADE UP OF?

The universe is anything and everything that exists. The universe is still a mystery to scientists. The universe is made up almost entirely of hydrogen and helium, the two lightest elements. All the rest of the matter in the universe is very rare. Elements such as silicon, carbon, and others are concentrated into clouds, stars, and planets. The universe is held together by four invisible forces. Gravity and electromagnetism are the two familiar forces. The other two are strong and weak nuclear forces. These operate only inside the incredibly tiny nuclei of atoms, holding the tiny particles together.

FACT FILE

Nobody knows exactly how big the universe is, what shape it is, where it came from, or what it will become. If we could go far enough into space, we might be able to understand more.

WHAT IS A DIFFUSE NEBULA?

Nebulae, which are clouds of dust and gas, come in many diferent shapes and sizes. Diffuse nebulae are extremely large structures, often many light-years wide, that have no definite outline and have a sketchy, cloud-like appearance. They are either luminous or dark. Diffuse nebulae shine because of the light of adjacent stars. They include some of the most striking objects in the sky, such as the Great Nebula in Orion. There are many thousands of luminous nebulae in our solar system.

FACT FILE

Dark nebulae appear dark because there are no nearby stars to light them. They can be observed because they blot out the light from more distant stars.

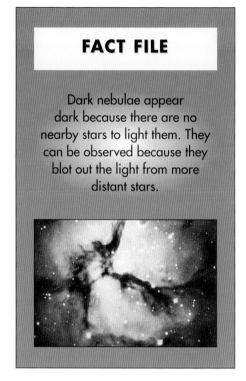

Orion nebula

WHAT IS THE KUIPER BELT?

An astronomer by the name of Gerard Kuiper suggested that beyond Neptune lay a belt of celestial bodies made up of rock and ice. Astronomers now think that there may be as many as 100,000 large, comet-like objects in the Kuiper Belt, including the planet Pluto. The icy bodies in the Kuiper Belt are called minor members, or "Plutinos," because they act like little Plutos. They are very difficult to see from Earth, even with the most powerful telescopes. If all the objects in the Kuiper Belt were joined together, they would form a planet the size of Earth.

FACT FILE

An object in space can be pulled into a spherical shape if its gravitational force is strong enough. Because the objects in the Kuiper Belt do not have powerful gravitational pulls, they come in all shapes and sizes.

WHICH PLANET IS ALWAYS DARK AND COLD?

On Pluto, it is always dark and cold, even in the middle of the day. This is because the sun appears 1,000 times fainter from the surface of Pluto than it does from Earth. It is little more than a faint star. In summer, Pluto has a slight atmosphere because the surface warms up enough to melt some of its ice, turning it to gas. As Pluto moves away from the sun, the gas freezes and becomes ice again. This means that in winter, Pluto's weather doesn't just get worse, it completely disappears.

FACT FILE

Little is known about Pluto's atmosphere, but it probably consists primarily of nitrogen with some carbon monoxide and methane.

WHAT IS THE NAME OF PLUTO'S MOON?

In 1978, Pluto was found to have a companion moon, which scientists named Charon. The moon is one third the size of Pluto, making it the biggest moon in comparison to its parent planet in the entire solar system. Pluto and Charon are only 12,430 miles (20,000 km) apart and are caught in a gravitational headlock, forming what scientists call a dual planet system. Nobody knows how Charon came to be Pluto's moon. Some believe Charon is made up of ice chipped off Pluto during a collision.

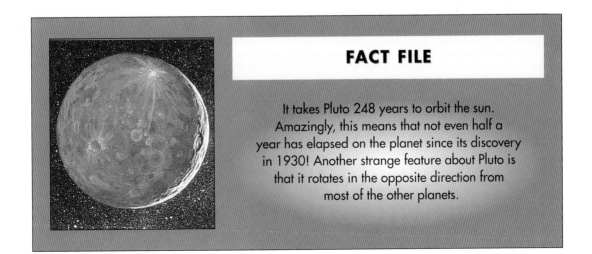

FACT FILE

It takes Pluto 248 years to orbit the sun. Amazingly, this means that not even half a year has elapsed on the planet since its discovery in 1930! Another strange feature about Pluto is that it rotates in the opposite direction from most of the other planets.

WHAT ARE MAGELLANIC CLOUDS?

The two galaxies that are closest to our own galaxy, the Milky Way, are the Magellanic Clouds, visible as faint areas of light in the night sky in the southern hemishere. Because the arrangement of stars within them does not follow a regular pattern, they are classified by astronomers as irregular galaxies.

They appear cloudy to the naked eye because, although they include billions of stars, individual stars in these galaxies can be seen only with the use of the most powerful telescopes.

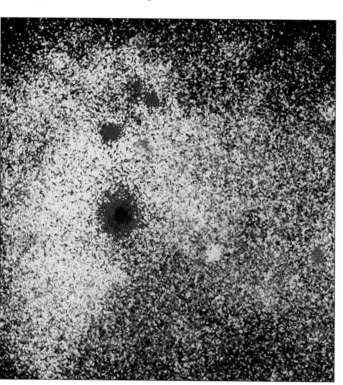

The Magellanic Clouds consist of an enormous quantity of gas, which is mostly composed of hydrogen. New stars are continually being formed from this gas. Much of the light that emanates from the Magellanic Clouds originates from the young, hot blue stars that are surrounded by luminous clouds of this gas.

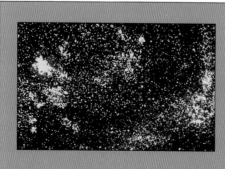

FACT FILE

Magellanic Couds were first recorded in the early 1500s during the circumglobal voyage of the Portuguese explorer Ferdinand Magellan, after whom they were named.

WHAT IS A SOLAR WIND?

The sun is constantly throwing off charged particles. They are known as the *solar wind*. Solar wind is strongest when sunspot activity is at its height. When the solar wind reaches the earth's magnetic field, the charged particles interact with gases in the earth's atmosphere 6 miles (10 km) above the surface. This interaction causes the particles to send out light, which is seen from earth as an amazing lightshow, most visible within the polar circles. In the northern hemisphere, this is known as the *aurora borealis*. In the southern hemisphere, it is called the *aurora australis*.

FACT FILE

Dark areas on the surface of the sun are called *sunspots*. These areas of cooler gas occur when the sun's magnetic field blocks the flow of heat from the core.

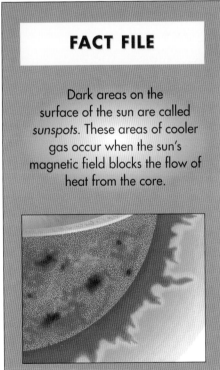

155

WHERE IS CALLISTO?

Larger than the planet Pluto and almost as big as Mercury, Callisto is a large moon of the planet Jupiter. It is one of the most heavily cratered bodies in the solar system. More than 4 billion years of bombardment from asteroids and comets has left its icy surface covered with craters of all sizes. The greatest impacts have formed enormous bulls-eye shapes in the cracked surface of the moon.

It has a surface covered by dark dirt that has been built up as icy crater rims and cliffs which have disintegrated over the passing eons. Callisto's carbon dioxide atmosphere is not much denser than that of the near-vacuum found in outer space.

FACT FILE

Callisto was discovered by the Italian astronomer Galileo in 1610. With a diameter of 2,986 miles (4,806 km), it orbits Jupiter every 16.7 days from a distance of 1,170,000 miles (1,883,000 km).

WHERE IS THERE A MOON OF ICE?

Another of Jupiter's large moons is Europa, with a surface layer of ice 50 to 100 miles (80 to 160 km) deep. It may have an ocean of water lying underneath it, which could be an environment for living beings. With an extremely thin atmosphere, the satellite is continuously bombarded by electrically charged particles from the radiation belts of Jupiter. The surface of Europa is one of the smoothest in the solar system. Its main features consist of shallow cracks, valleys, blisters, ridges, pits, and icy flows, none of which are more than a few hundred meters in height or depth. Here and there large portions of the surface have split from each other. This is why Europa has few impact craters. Most of the old craters have been destroyed by this splitting and shifting of the surface and by the disruptions from below.

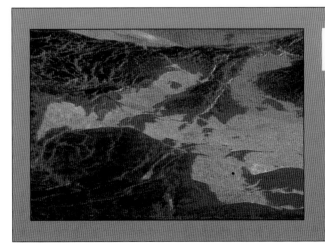

FACT FILE

The internal heat of Europa, which is hotter than that at the surface, is a result of the gravitational forces of Jupiter and Jupiter's other large satellites. This pulls the satellite's interior in opposing directions.

WHERE DO ASTEROIDS COME FROM?

Also called a minor planet or planetoid, an asteroid is one of numerous small planetary bodies that revolve around the sun. They are mostly found in the asteroid belt, which lies between the orbits of Mars and Jupiter. This belt contains more than 1,150 asteroids with diameters greater than eighteen miles (30 km).

Although astronomers are not sure how the asteroids originated, the most popular theory is that they were left over from when the planets were first formed. They are the shattered remnants of a smaller group of larger objects.

FACT FILE

Most asteroids drift harmlessly in their orbits around the sun. Occasionally, an asteroid may be knocked out of its orbit and sent on a collision course with a planet.

WHERE IS THERE A GIANT BALL OF GAS?

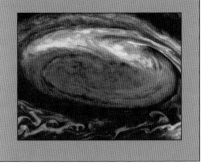

Jupiter, the largest planet in the solar system, is a giant ball of gas and liquid. It has little, if any, solid surface. Its diameter is 88,846 miles (142,984 km), more than 11 times that of Earth, and about one-tenth that of the sun. The planet's surface is mainly composed of dense red, brown, yellow, and white clouds.

In 1995, the Galileo space probe dropped a smaller probe into the churning, turbulent atmosphere of the gas giant. It took measurements for almost an hour before it was destroyed by the massive planet's great atmospheric pressure.

WHERE IS THE OLYMPUS MONS?

Mars is the only planet whose surface can be seen in detail from Earth. Mars has one of the most striking surfaces of any planet in the solar system. Giant volcanoes tower above its landscape. The largest of these is the Olympus Mons, which is 15.5 miles (25 km) tall, three times taller than Mount Everest. Mars is also home to Valles Marineris, a canyon that is 112 miles (180 km) wide, up to 4.3 miles (7 km) deep, and long enough to stretch across the United States.

Mars does not have water on its surface now, but there is evidence that there were rivers and seas on Mars in the past. Probes have taken many pictures of the planet's surface, and scientists have identified several channels that could have been formed only by running water. Astronomers believe that there was a great deal of liquid water on Mars billions of years ago.

FACT FILE

In 1996, scientists produced evidence that proved that living creatures inhabited Mars more than 3.6 billion years ago.

WHERE ARE
METEOR SHOWERS SEEN?

At certain times every year, the earth comes in contact with a number of trails, called *streams*, or clusters, called *showers*, of tiny meteoroids. The sky looks as if it is filled with a shower of sparks. Believed to be fragments of comets, these trails and clusters have similar orbits to those of comets.

The most brilliant meteor shower ever known was one of the Leonid showers that occurred on November 12-13, 1833. These showers occur every November and come from the direction of the constellation Leo.

FACT FILE

Barringer Crater is a huge depression in the earth in north central Arizona. It measures about 4,180 ft. (1,275 m) wide and 570 ft. (175 m) deep. It was formed about 50,000 years ago when a meteorite struck the earth.

SPACE

TECHNOLOGY

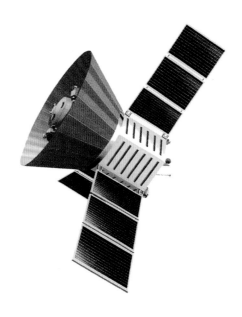

CONTENTS

WHAT IS A SPACE SHUTTLE?

A space shuttle is a reusable spacecraft. It was developed to provide a reusable, and therefore cheaper, vehicle for launching satellites into space. The shuttle is a bulky, delta-winged aircraft with powerful rocket motors. At launch, two solid-fuel booster rockets are strapped to its sides, and a giant fuel tank is attached to its underside. The rockets and fuel tank fall away after launch, and the rockets are recovered and reused. In orbit, the shuttle's cargo bay opens to release satellites or to allow the crew to work in space. The shuttle lands on a runway like a conventional airplane.

Launching a space shuttle

FACT FILE

At takeoff, the space shuttle weighs 2,200 tons (2,000 tonnes). It burns almost all of its fuel in the first few minutes after launch, then continues to coast into its orbit 186 mi. (300 km) above the surface of the earth.

WHAT ARE THE BENEFITS OF SPACE EXPLORATION?

Leaving the launch pad

FACT FILE

The Hubble Space telescope was launched in 1990 as a revolutionary piece of equipment for astronomers. It is able to focus on objects not visible to the human eye.

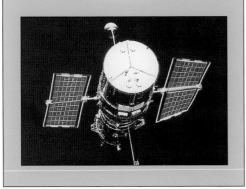

Until 1957, human beings were just observers of the solar system. Now, they have entered the realm of space and gathered first-hand knowledge of their planetary environment. Twelve men have landed on the moon, set up data-gathering experiments on the lunar surface, and brought back lunar rocks and soil for study and analysis. The hidden side of the moon and the planets Mercury, Venus, Mars, Jupiter, and Saturn have been photographed and studied. The earth and its weather have been studied, and communication relays and navigational aids have been established.

WHAT DO SPACE SATELLITES DO?

Space satellites have revolutionized communications, making everyday developments, such as mobile phones and television, possible. Communication satellites receive signals beamed at them from the earth and send them on to other places. They transmit television and telephone signals around the world, even to remote areas. They are also used for defense communications, including checking on the movement of military forces. Satellites can survey the earth's surface, predict weather changes, and track hurricanes. They can also examine resources such as crops, forests, and even minerals.

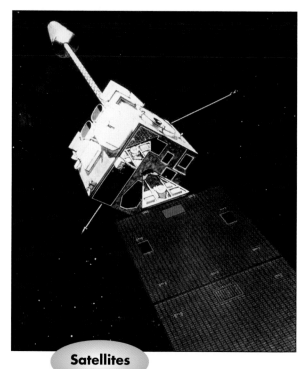

Satellites

FACT FILE

Navigation satellites enable people on land or at sea to work out their exact map position within a few feet.

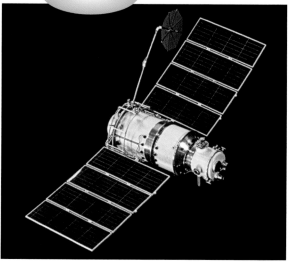

HOW DID WE BENEFIT FROM THE DISCOVERY OF INFRARED?

Sir Frederick William Herschel (1738–1822) was born in Germany and became well-known as both a musician and an astronomer. Herschel's

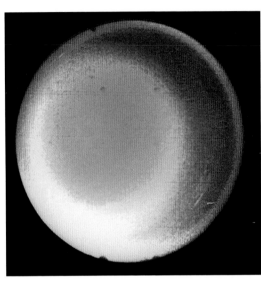

experiments with light proved to be important, not only because it led to the discovery of infrared, but also because it was the first time that someone proved there were forms of light that we cannot see with our eyes. Today, infrared technology has many exciting and useful applications. In the field of infrared astronomy, new and fascinating discoveries are being made about the universe. Medical infrared imaging is a very useful diagnostic tool. Infrared cameras are used for police and security work as well as in fire-fighting and in the military. Infrared imaging is used to detect heat loss in buildings and to test electronic systems. Infrared satellites have been used to monitor the earth's weather, to study vegetation patterns, and to study geology and ocean temperatures.

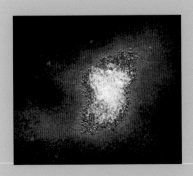

FACT FILE

Ultraviolet and X-ray astronomy are radiation sources of a higher energy level than infrared. They are best observed by telescopes orbiting earth's atmosphere. Ultraviolet astronomy is used to track down the hottest stars.

WHEN WAS THE FIRST WEATHER SATELLITE LAUNCHED?

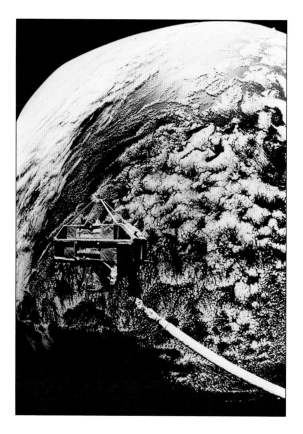

Forty years ago, predicting the weather was about as accurate as guessing who would win the lottery. In the days before television forecasts, weather monitoring was limited to wind, temperature, and rainfall gauges aboard airplanes, balloons, and ships.

All that changed on April 1, 1960, when the government launched the first weather satellite, called *TIROS 1*, into orbit from Cape Canaveral, Florida. It paved the way for generations of weather satellites that today do everything from monitoring crops to tracking the movement of mosquitoes across continents.

FACT FILE

Thanks to the Internet, meteorologists can view high-resolution satellite images of incoming storms, and can give coastal areas enough advance warning to evacuate.

WHAT DO ASTRONAUTS EAT IN SPACE?

FACT FILE

The shuttle menu is repeated each seven days. It supplies each crew member with three balanced meals, plus snacks.

Early astronauts found the task of eating in space fairly easy, but the menu was limited. They had to endure bite-sized cubes, freeze-dried powders, and semi-liquids stuffed in metal tubes.

With improved packaging came improved food quality. Gemini astronauts had food choices such as shrimp cocktail, chicken and vegetables, butterscotch pudding, and applesauce. They were able to select meal combinations themselves.

With improved technology, the quality and variety of food became even better. Apollo astronauts were the first to have hot water, which made rehydrating foods easier and improved the food's taste. These astronauts were also the first to use the "spoon bowl," a plastic container that could be opened and eaten with a spoon.

WHAT TYPE OF TRAINING DOES AN ASTRONAUT NEED?

Astronaut candidates are carefully screened to meet the highest physical and mental standards, and they undergo rigorous training. As much as is

possible, all conditions that will be encountered in space are simulated in ground training. Astronauts are trained to function effectively in cramped quarters while wearing restrictive space suits. Their reactions during liftoff are tested during simulation. They are prepared for the disorientation of weightlessness, and they spend long periods in isolation chambers to test their psychological reactions to solitude. Using trainers and mock-ups of actual spacecraft, astronauts rehearse every exercise from liftoff to recovery, and every conceivable malfunction and difficulty is anticipated and prepared for.

FACT FILE

In addition to flight training, astronauts are required to have a thorough knowledge of all aspects of space science, such as celestial mechanics and rocketry.

WHY DO ASTRONAUTS EXERCISE IN SPACE?

Because muscles do not have to fight against gravity in space, they can waste away from lack of use. This means that astronauts must exercise every day. Conditions in space can be very strange. There is almost no gravity inside a space station, which means that astronauts can float in midair and lift heavy objects effortlessly. This lack of gravity can be a problem. Scientists in space stations have to strap themselves to the walls while they are working to keep from floating away. Also, there is no regular night or day on a space station. For example, on Mir the sun rises and sets every ninety minutes.

FACT FILE

Studies showing how astronauts could walk in the moon's weak gravitational field led to a deeper understanding of human locomotion.

HOW DO ASTRONAUTS MOVE AROUND IN SPACE?

FACT FILE

In an emergency, backpacks enable tumbling astronauts to right themselves and travel back to safety at a rate of about 10 ft. (3 m) per second.

Astronauts often have to repair components of satellites or space stations. Movement in space can be very difficult and risky. Microgravity means that an astronaut is in danger of floating away or losing a vital tool into outer space. Handles and special footholds, into which feet can be locked, help astronauts move around in space. When they have to fly further away from their shuttles, astronauts use special backpacks that have rockets built into them. These backpacks are a little like floating armchairs and are directed by a handheld device like a joystick. These backpacks are powered by 24 nitrogen gas thrusters.

WHAT ARE SPACE SUITS MADE OF?

Space suits are made of specially adapted man-made materials, such as urethane-coated nylon. Designing a space suit is a very complex procedure, because it needs to give the astronaut complete control and protection. The space suit also needs to act like a miniature spacecraft. It provides everything that an astronaut needs to survive for short periods in space. This includes oxygen to breathe, water to drink, heating and cooling devices, communication apparatus, and toilet facilities. These suits have been developed to withstand the extreme conditions of space.

FACT FILE

The space suit maintains a constant air pressure by surrounding the body with a kind of balloon. This balloon is full of air and presses against the body in the same way as the earth's atmosphere.

HOW DOES A SPACE SHUTTLE LEAVE EARTH?

Like other spacecraft, the shuttle is launched from a vertical position. Liftoff thrust is obtained from the orbiter's three main engines and the boosters. After two minutes, the boosters use up all their fuel and separate from the spacecraft. They are recovered following splashdown with the aid of attached parachutes. After about eight minutes of flight, the orbiter's main engines shut down. Then, the external tank is jettisoned and burned up as it re-enters the atmosphere. Meanwhile, the orbiter enters orbit after a short burn of its two small Orbiting Maneuvering System (OMS) engines. To return to earth, the orbiter turns around, fires its OMS engines to reduce speed, and after descending through the atmosphere, lands like a glider.

FACT FILE

Following four orbital test flights of the space shuttle Columbia between 1981 and 1982, operational flights began in November 1982.

Columbia space shuttle

WHAT IS A GEOSTATIONARY SATELLITE?

There are two types of weather satellites for long- and short-term observations. Together they give a complete picture of earth's weather system.

Geostationary operational environmental satellites take real-time photographs of various regions of the earth. They predicts floods, hurricanes, thunderstorms, and other severe weather patterns as quickly as possible with the help of radars and other ground systems. A polar-

orbiting environmental satellite offers a larger, more long-term picture of the environment. Snapping visible and infrared photographs that measure temperature and moisture, these satellites track patterns affecting the weather and climate of the world.

Satellite's view of earth

FACT FILE

These satellites also carry search-and-rescue transmission instruments so that aircraft and ships in distress can relay messages through them for help.

HOW DO SATELLITES MONITOR VOLCANOES?

Scientists can now analyze weather-satellite pictures to monitor 100 dangerous, remote volcanoes along the Pacific Rim in Alaska and Russia. They are looking for excess heat that indicates that a volcano is likely to erupt. The method allows scientists to observe volcanoes when it is too expensive to install earthquake sensors to listen for signs of imminent eruptions.

Only 27 volcanoes in Alaska and Russia are monitored seismically because reaching these remote locations is difficult and costly. Long periods of winter darkness render solar-powered monitoring stations useless, and the extreme cold makes batteries inefficient. So for the past few years, scientists have routinely examined infrared images taken by weather satellites.

FACT FILE

The heat-sensing satellites not only help predict eruptions, they also monitor eruptions in progress. Scientists use the pictures to track volcanic ash and observe lava flows and lava domes.

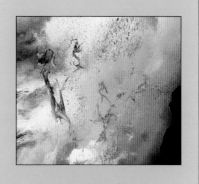

ARE THERE REALLY UFOS?

UFO stands for *unidentified flying object*, which refers to a light or object seen in the air that cannot be explained. Although there are people who believe that UFOs are vehicles flown by aliens from other planets, most UFO sightings are eventually explained by the accounts of reliable witnesses. In fact, many reported UFOs are normal astronomical objects, such as meteors, comets, or even very bright stars or planets. Aircraft, missiles, satellites, weather balloons, as well as birds and insect swarms, have all been mistaken for UFOs. Unusual weather conditions can also create optical illusions thought to be UFOs.

All but a very small percentage of UFO reports are explained by investigators. Those that are not explained may be due to some unknown factor or limitations in human perception and memory. Most scientists think that there is simply not enough evidence to link UFOs with visitors from other planets.

FACT FILE

The term "flying saucer," which is used for many UFOs, first appeared in the press in 1947 to describe a sighting by airplane pilot Kenneth Arnold. He reported weird, saucer-like objects speeding through the air.

HOW MANY COMMUNICATIONS SATELLITES ARE IN ORBIT?

There are hundreds of active communications satellites now in orbit. Communications satellites were originally designed to operate in a passive mode. Instead of actively transmitting radio signals, they served merely to reflect signals that were beamed up to them by transmitting stations on the ground. Signals were reflected in all directions, so they could be picked up by receiving stations around the world. *Echo 1*, an early satellite launched by the United States in 1960, consisted of an aluminized plastic balloon 100 ft. (30 m) in diameter. Launched in 1964, *Echo 2* was 135 ft. (41 m) in diameter. The capacity of such systems was severely limited by the need for powerful transmitters and large ground antennae.

Morelos-B

FACT FILE

The first long-distance phone call was made in Canada in 1886. A century later, Canada was the first country to set up a satellite network. Satellites now provide a vital link to many remote communities.

How does space research help us in daily life?

Scientists not only study living organisms in space, they can also study combustion in microgravity to help design more efficient jet engines. The study of crystal growth has helped us to build better semiconductors for computers. Everyone has benefitted from technology that was designed for use in space. Microchips, that are found in everything from digital watches to computers, were first developed so that a lot of equipment could fit into a small spacecraft. Advancements such as keyhole surgery, solar power, as well as ordinary household items like Velcro, air-tight cans, and kitchen foil have all developed as a result of space research and technology.

FACT FILE

Astronomers today hardly ever use telescopes. Instead, a telescope sends an image to a photographic plate or to an electronic light-sensitive computer chip called a *charge-coupled device*, or CCD. CCDs are about 50 times more sensitive than film, so today's astronomers can record in a minute an image that would have taken about an hour to record on film.

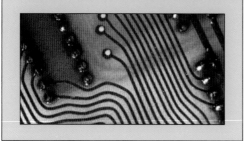

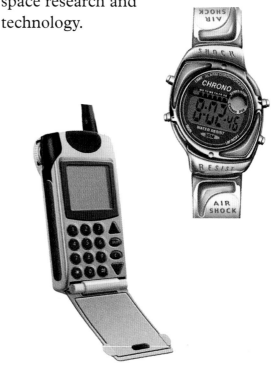

WHAT IS THE LARGEST TELESCOPE IN THE WORLD?

Two identical telescopes, called *Keck I* and *Keck II*, are the largest reflecting telescopes in the world. Each has a segmented mirror that is 33 ft. (10 m) in diameter. The telescopes are on Mauna Kea, a mountain in Hawaii.

The telescopes are in an observatory that stands under a large dome with shutters. The dome and the shutters protect the telescopes from the weather. Motors and precision gears keep the telescopes pointed in the desired direction as the earth rotates. Observatories use two principal kinds of optical telescopes–reflecting telescopes and refracting telescopes. Reflecting telescopes use a curved mirror to focus light, while refracting telescopes use a system of lenses.

FACT FILE

Refracting telescopes need thick lenses for high magnification. The refracting telescope at the Yerkes Observatory in Williams Bay, Wisconsin, has the world's largest lens. It measures 40 in. (102 cm) in diameter.

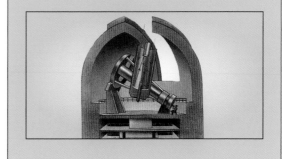

WHO BUILT THE FIRST WORKING ROCKET?

According to historians, the Chinese built the first working rockets. They were also the first to use them for military purposes. In 1232 A.D., an ingenious military leader used arrows powered by small gunpowder rockets to successfully defend the city of K'ai-Fung-Foo from the invading Mongols.

During this time, one Chinese official came up with the idea of using rockets to propel a man through the air. It was around 1500 A.D. that Wan Hu rigged a pair of kites together with a chair attached in between. He then tied a series of military rockets to the kites and asked a group of servants to light the rockets. Not wanting to miss out on the chance for fame, Wan Hu decided to be his own test pilot. According to reports, he sat in the chair and gave the order to light the rockets. There was a lot of noise and a great burst of flame and smoke, which blocked everyone's vision. When the smoke cleared, Wan Hu was gone!

FACT FILE

In 1931, Johannes Winkler launched an HW-1 rocket. It went 6 feet into the air, turned over, and fell back to the ground.

HOW DO ASTRONAUTS TRAVEL ON THE MOON?

In later Apollo missions, astronauts took the lunar rover, or moon buggy, with them. This enabled them to explore further than had ever been possible. Equipment on board the buggy included a television camera and a satellite dish so that pictures could be sent back to earth. To avoid damage from the rough surface of the moon, the tires were solid. Steering was controlled by a small handheld control, rather than a wheel. The lunar rover was powered by a battery. Its top speed was just under 12 mph (20 km/h). It carried tool kits and bags to hold samples.

FACT FILE

Altogether, there have been six Apollo missions to the moon. Twelve astronauts have explored its conditions and composition. They have tested the soil to determine what the moon is made of and have also measured moonquakes.

WHY DO FOOTPRINTS STAY ON THE MOON FOREVER?

The footprints left by Apollo astronauts will last for centuries because there is no wind on the moon. The flag the Americans left behind on the moon is held out with a metal bar because there is no wind to allow it to fly.

The moon does not have an atmosphere, so there is no weather like we have on earth. Because there is no atmosphere to trap heat, the temperatures on the moon vary dramatically over the course of a day, from 212°F (100°C) at noon to -279°F (–173° C) at night. The moon has no rain, wind, or earthquakes to wear away or break down the craters. So, they have remained the same for millions of years.

The moon does not produce its own light, but looks bright because it reflects light from the sun. Think of the sun as a lightbulb and the moon as a mirror, reflecting light from the lightbulb. The lunar phase changes as the moon orbits the earth and different portions of its surface are illuminated by the sun.

FACT FILE

Sometimes, the moon appears orange. This occurs when there is a lot of dust, smoke, or pollution in the atmosphere. The size of those particles will determine what you see. Sometimes, the moon will look red, orange, or even blue.

WHERE IS THE HUBBLE TELESCOPE IN ORBIT?

The Hubble space telescope is a powerful telescope orbiting 380 miles (610 km) above the earth. It provides sharper images of heavenly bodies than other telescopes do. It is a reflecting telescope with a light-gathering mirror 94 inches (240 cm) in diameter. The telescope is named after American astronomer Edwin P. Hubble, who made significant contributions to astronomy in the 1920s. The Hubble space telescope views the skies without looking through the earth's atmosphere. The atmosphere bends light due to a phenomenon known as *diffraction*. The atmosphere is constantly moving. This combination of diffraction and movement causes starlight to bounce around as it passes through the air, making the stars appear to twinkle.

FACT FILE

Radio observatories have radio telescopes to study radio waves. Most radio telescopes use large antennae to capture radio waves from space. In most cases, computers guide the telescopes and analyze the data they collect.

WHERE WAS THE FIRST COMET IMPACT OBSERVED?

The space shuttle Discovery launched a telescope into orbit in 1990. Soon after the launch, engineers discovered a flaw in the telescope's light-gathering mirror. The flaw made the images less clear than they otherwise would have been. Engineers designed an optical device to bend light reflected by the mirror in a way that would make up for this error. Astronauts from the space shuttle Endeavour installed the device on the telescope in 1993, and it worked as planned.

Along with many other telescopes, the Hubble space telescope observed Jupiter being bombarded with fragments of comet Shoemaker-

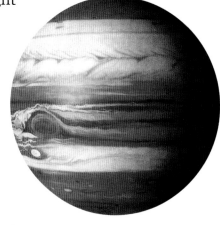

Levy 9 in 1994. The images showed astonishing holes in Jupiter's atmosphere where the comet pieces smashed through. This bombardment was the first comet impact ever observed as it happened.

FACT FILE

The Viking probe visited Mars in 1976 in search of life. They conducted numerous tests on Martian soils but found no evidence of any living organisms.

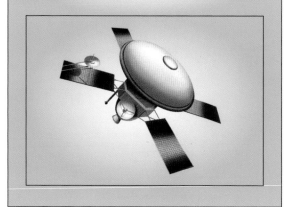

WHY ARE SPACE STATIONS NEEDED?

Space stations are usually made up of several modules that are sent into orbit one at a time and then assembled once in space. Space stations allow the crew to work in space for long periods of time in conditions of zero gravity. While conditions in space capsules and space shuttles are cramped, space stations are designed for longer stays in space. A rocket or a space shuttle brings air and food supplies to the space station, along with a replacement crew.

Some space stations, such as the Russian Mir, stayed up for many years, and their crews remained in space for months at a time.

Mir space station

FACT FILE

Blow up a balloon and let it go without tying a knot in its neck. The air will rush out very quickly. When the air comes out, it pushes the balloon upward, just like a rocket!

WHY ARE PROBES IMPORTANT IN SPACE EXPLORATION?

Space probes are small packages of instruments that are launched from Earth to explore the planets. Probes have landed small instrument capsules on Mars and Venus. These instruments take photographs or test the atmosphere of a planet. Some probes use the gravity of other planets to extend their voyages. They pass close by a planet, using its gravity to swing around it to hurl towards another planet. Using this technique, the Voyager 2 space probe was able to visit Jupiter, Saturn, Uranus, and Neptune. Probes do not have their own rocket power apart from tiny thrusters for steering.

FACT FILE

Neil Armstrong became the first man to walk on the moon on July 20, 1969.

FURTHER

FACTS

CONTENTS

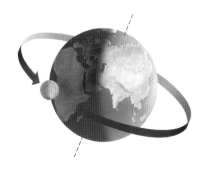

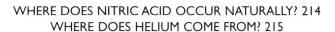

WHY DO WE NEED OIL?

Fossil fuels, which include oil, coal, and natural gas, were formed millions of years ago when prehistoric plants and animals died. Their decaying bodies were pressed under layers of rock and earth and became fossilized. Life would not be possible without fossil fuels. Fossil fuels are burned to supply heat and energy to our homes and industry. They also form the fuel for power stations and supply most of the electricity we use. Fossil fuels can be processed to produce other useful materials, such as plastics, dyes, and bitumen.

Geologists know what kinds of rocks are likely to contain or cover oil deposits. When they find a likely source, they test-drill to find out if there is any oil beneath the surface.

FACT FILE

Helicopters are an oil rig's lifeline. They not only bring workers food and supplies, but they can also airlift an injured worker to the hospital.

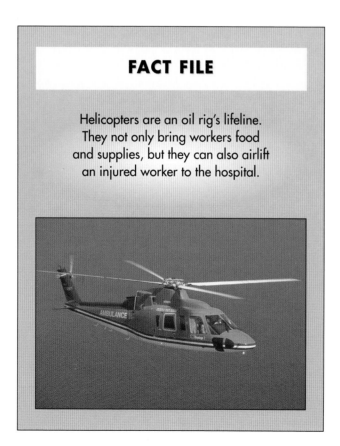

Drill

WHY DO OIL RIGS CATCH FIRE?

Living quarters

Platform

Oil well

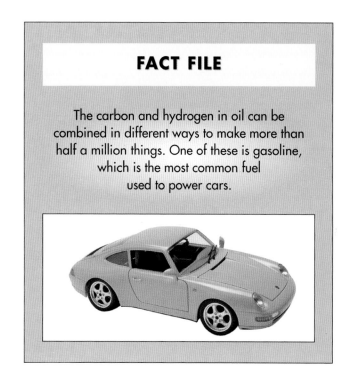

FACT FILE

The carbon and hydrogen in oil can be combined in different ways to make more than half a million things. One of these is gasoline, which is the most common fuel used to power cars.

Much of the world's oil is found buried beneath the sea. Oil rigs are large floating devices that are anchored to the seabed. Workers drill wells into the oil-bearing rocks. These self-contained rigs hold all of the drilling machinery and a helicopter pad to receive supplies.

When the oil is extracted from the rock, it contains a large amount of gas, which has to be burned off at the surface. The gas gushing from an oil well can have great force. If this should become ignited, the resulting fire burns far too fiercely to be put out with water or fire extinguishers. Instead, firefighters use a special crane to position an explosive device in the flames. It may seem strange to fight a fire with an explosion, but when this explosion occurs, it uses the surrounding oxygen, temporarily depriving the fire of oxygen and thus putting it out.

WHY IS STEEL IMPORTANT?

Iron has a lot of carbon in it, which makes it crack very easily. If some carbon is removed, iron turns into super-strong steel. A great range of items are made of steel, from tiny paperclips to large girders, forming the frames for skyscrapers. One very useful property of steel is that it can be recycled. Steel is the most important ingredient for making cars. Most screws, nails, nuts, and bolts are made of steel. The large cranes that make modern construction possible are built of steel.

FACT FILE

Stainless steel contains small amounts of nickel and chromium to make a metal that does not corrode. Many everyday things are made of stainless steel, such as silverware, sewing pins and needles, and scissors.

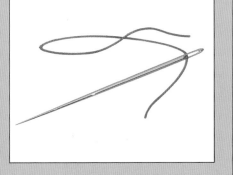

WHAT ARE BLAST FURNACES?

Iron is the most widely used of all metals. It is cheap and strong, so it is used to make the supports for huge buildings and bridges. *Smelting* is a reduction reaction. It is a method of extracting iron from iron ore. The process of smelting takes place in something called a *blast furnace*, (pictured above). The blast furnace gets its name from the hot air that is blasted into it. This is where iron ore, limestone, and coke (a form of carbon) are heated together while hot air is blasted into the furnace. The carbon in the coke reacts with the oxygen in the air to form carbon monoxide. This, in turn, takes oxygen from the iron ore, leaving behind iron mixed with a little carbon. The temperature inside the furnaces reaches 3632°F (2000°C).

FACT FILE

Alloys of steel, in which steel is combined with other metals, can be very useful. Railway tracks are made from an alloy of steel and manganese.

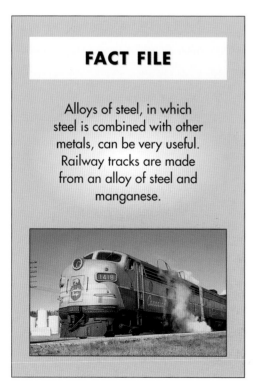

WHAT IS A SUNDIAL?

The first concept of time that human beings had came from watching the sun as it moved across the sky. They found that shadows cast by the sun could give a clearer, more accurate idea of the time than looking directly at the sun. From this concept, the first sundials were invented.

The first sundials were probably very primitive, just poles stuck into the ground with the shadow's position marked with stones. Sundials have been used for many centuries and continue to be used today.

FACT FILE

After the sundials were invented, other means of telling the time were developed for the indoors, such as hourglasses and burning candles. The invention of clocks permitted far more accurate timekeeping.

A sundial

WHY DO WE NEED TO MEASURE TIME?

People have always organized their lives according to time. The earliest hunters had to hunt during daylight. When farming developed, it was important for farmers to understand the seasons in order to plant their crops at the right time. Long ago, people realized that the movement of the sun allowed them to recognize the time of day.

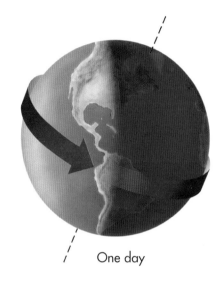

One day

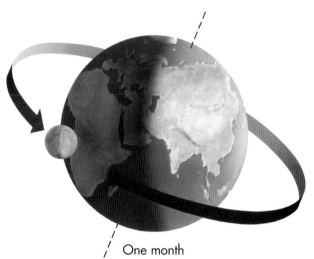

One month

People also realized that the movement of the moon was regular. They discovered it could be used to give measurements of roughly one month. Modern life is governed much more by time, as we now depend on highly accurate clocks to measure every second of the day.

FACT FILE

Modern clocks are often digital. These clocks contain electronic circuits that receive digital signals in binary code.

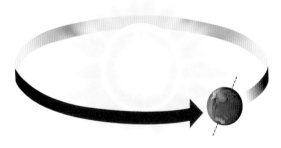

One year

WHY IS FIRE SO HOT?

Fire is a chemical reaction that takes place very quickly and gives off light and heat. This is usually a reaction between oxygen and some sort of fuel. If heat and light are produced, fire results. There are three things necessary to create a fire: fuel, oxygen, and heat. If there is a combustible like wood or paper present, simply exposing it to the air does not mean it will catch fire. Fuel must be added.

When the fuel becomes hot enough, it will ignite and burst into flames as oxygen combines with it. There is a particular temperature at which every fuel begins to burn, known as the *kindling temperature*, or the *flash point*, of the fuel.

When something catches fire, it is important to bring the flames under control as soon as possible. This is especially true when a building catches fire.

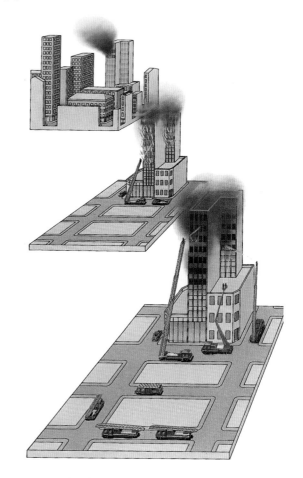

FACT FILE

Firefighters must wear protective clothing that does not conduct heat easily so it will not catch fire easily. Fireproof clothing often has a shiny surface, because this helps to reflect the radiated heat away from the body.

HOW CAN WAX BE BOTH NATURAL AND SYNTHETIC?

We get wax from a number of different sources. It can be acquired from natural plant sources in fruit and vegetables. Waxes can also be found in oil and minerals.

For instance, the brown carnauba wax, which is used in records, floor dressings, and candles is obtained from the leaves of the carnauba palm tree of Brazil. Likewise, bayberry wax, which we get from the

berries of the shrub, is also used in making candles.

Even bees making their honeycombs use a wax which they secrete. This is used to make a variety of goods from artificial flowers and candles, to crayons and household polishes.

A wax obtained from wool-bearing animals, called *lanolin*, is used to make cosmetics and soap.

The most commonly used wax is petroleum wax, which is odorless, tasteless, and chemically inactive. It accounts for over 90 percent of all commercial waxes in use today.

FACT FILE

Inside a hive, bees store their honey in a network of wax, which is called a *honeycomb*. Each one is made up of thousands of little six-sided cells. The bees feed on the honey in the winter months.

WHY DO BOATS HAVE SAILS?

Nearly three-quarters of the earth's surface is covered by water. Most of this water is in the seas and oceans. For thousands of years, people have been finding ways to cross this water. At first, they built rafts and boats with oars, but around 2900 B.C., the Egyptians began to use sails. From then on, sailing ships ruled the seas until about a century ago. Today, big ships have engines, but small sailing ships are used for sport, fishing, and local trade.

Of course, sailing ships are dependent on wind to power them. Sailors are unable to change the direction of the wind, but they can change the direction of their sailing boats by steering a zigzag course, called *tacking*.

FACT FILE

Yacht racing is a very popular sport. In yacht racing, it is often the efficiency with which a boat tacks, compared with its competitors, that makes it win.

WHY DO CARS HAVE ENGINES?

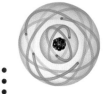

The first vehicle able to run on the open road was powered by steam. However, it was not until the development of the internal combustion engine in the second half of the nineteenth century that motor transportion began to be successful.

Internal combustion engines are usually fueled by gasoline or diesel fuel. This fuel is burned (or combusted) within metal cylinders. The burning fuel causes a piston to move up and down inside each cylinder. It is this upward and downward movement that is transferred into a turning movement by the crankshaft, causing the axles and wheels to turn and the car to move forward. The engine also powers an alternator, which generates electric current. This current is stored in the battery and is used for the car's lights, windshield wipers, radio, and features like electric windows.

The first gasoline-driven car

FACT FILE

Most gasoline engines are noisy and give off harmful fumes. Quieter and cleaner electric cars are now being designed. But their batteries need to be recharged so they are used only for short distances.

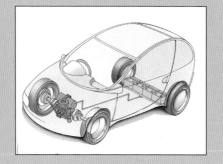

WHO WAS ARCHIMEDES?

Archimedes was a Greek mathematician who lived between about 287 and 212 B.C. Archimedes performed experiments to test his theories. He made practical inventions, such as the Archimedean screw, which is still used today to lift water for irrigation. He also worked out the laws which govern the use of levers and pulleys.

Perhaps the thing he is remembered most for is when he jumped out of his bath and ran through the streets shouting "Eureka!", which means

FACT FILE

Luigi Galvani (1737–1798) was an Italian scientist. He accidentally noticed that severed frogs' legs twitched when the nerve was touched with a pair of metal scissors during a thunderstorm.

"I've found it!" Whether this story is true or not, he did discover that an object displaces its own weight in water when floating or submerged.

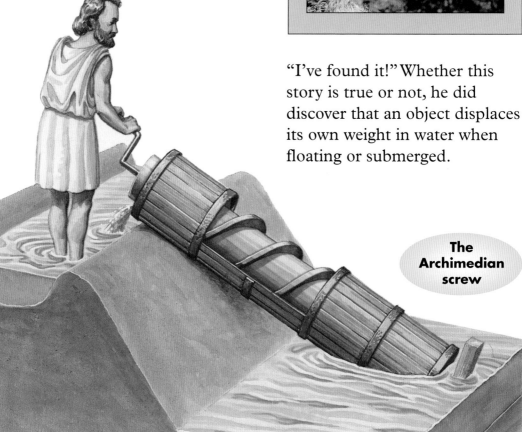

The Archimedian screw

WHY IS EINSTEIN REMEMBERED?

Albert Einstein (1879–1955) was a physicist who was born in Germany. He developed the theory of relativity, which led to the famous equation $E = mc^2$.

Einstein's work is the basis for most of the modern theories about nature, history, and the structure of the universe. He composed the rules that govern objects moving close to the speed of light and explained why travel at this sort of speed could distort time itself. His work also proved invaluable in the development of the atomic bomb. He is remembered as one of the greatest scientists of our time.

FACT FILE

Benjamin Franklin (1706–1790) had many talents. He was a printer, scientist, and politician who played an important part in founding the United States. He developed lightning rods to protect buildings from storms.

WHY WERE THE PYRAMID BUILDERS GOOD MATHEMATICIANS?

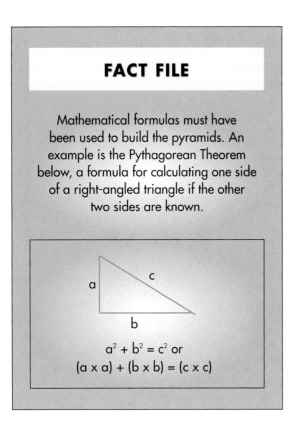

FACT FILE

Mathematical formulas must have been used to build the pyramids. An example is the Pythagorean Theorem below, a formula for calculating one side of a right-angled triangle if the other two sides are known.

$$a^2 + b^2 = c^2 \text{ or}$$
$$(a \times a) + (b \times b) = (c \times c)$$

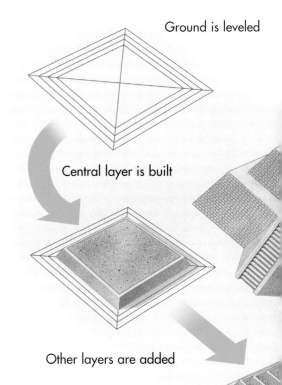

Ground is leveled

Central layer is built

Other layers are added

The Egyptians built massive pyramids almost 5,000 years ago. We are still not sure how they achieved this without the mechanical lifting and cutting equipment that we have today. The answer is that they probably used a large number of slaves to shape and haul the enormous stones they used to build with. Scientists have calculated that as many as 10,000 slaves were probably needed to work on one of these structures.

The shape of a pyramid, a three-dimensional figure with flat faces, is called a *polyhedron*. These huge structures were very carefully designed and constructed. It is clear that the builders must have had a good knowledge of mathematics in order to build and measure these vast pyramids with such accuracy.

WHY DO WE NEED NUMBERS?

The building of pyramids

Numbers are used to describe the amount of things. We can express numbers in words, by hand gestures, or in writing using symbols or numerals. When we talk about a number we use the word *five* rather than the numeral 5. When we write, we use both words and numerals.

Numbers can describe how many objects there are or an object's position among other objects.

Other types of numbers are used to describe how many units of something there are; for example, how many pounds (weight) or feet (length). Numbers are a convenient way of describing the amount of something.

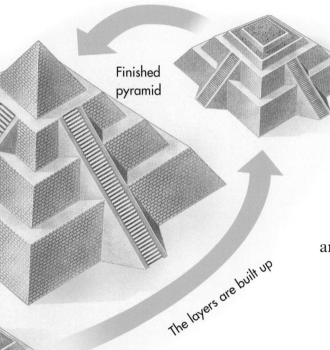

Finished pyramid

The layers are built up

FACT FILE

Roman numerals are still used today for certain purposes. They appear on watch and clock faces, and when numbers have a certain importance, such as in the title of a monarch.

I	1	IX	9
II	2	X	10
III	3	XX	20
IV	4	L	50
V	5	C	100
VI	6	M	1000
VII	7		
VIII	8		

HOW MANY DIFFERENT ELEMENTS ARE THERE?

There are 92 different elements that exist naturally, but scientists have been able to create many more in the laboratory. These artificial elements are radioactive and can quickly decay or lose their radioactivity. Some may exist for only a few seconds or less. Hydrogen is the lightest element, and uranium is the heaviest. New elements are created by bombarding other elements with radiation in an atomic reactor.

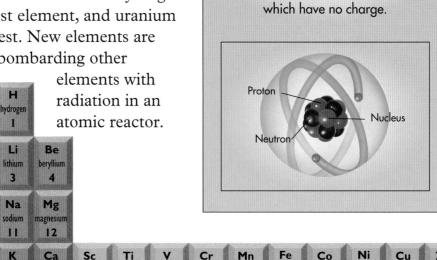

FACT FILE

At the center of an atom is its nucleus, which has shells of electrons around it. The nucleus consists of protons, which are electrically charged particles, and neutrons, which have no charge.

Proton

Nucleus

Neutron

H hydrogen 1												
Li lithium 3	Be beryllium 4												B boron 5
Na sodium 11	Mg magnesium 12												Al aluminium 13
K potassium 19	Ca calcium 20	Sc scandium 21	Ti titanium 22	V vanadium 23	Cr chromium 24	Mn manganese 25	Fe iron 26	Co cobalt 27	Ni nickel 28	Cu copper 29	Zn zinc 30	Ga gallium 31
Rb rubidium 37	Sr strontium 38	Y yttrium 39	Zr zirconium 40	Nb niobium 41	Mo molybdenum 42	Tc technetium 43	Ru ruthenium 44	Rh rhodium 45	Pd palladium 46	Ag silver 47	Cd cadmium 48	In indium 49
Cs caesium 55	Ba barium 56	Lu lutetium 71	Hf hafnium 72	Ta tantalum 73	W tungsten 74	Re rhenium 75	Os osmium 76	Ir iridium 77	Pt platinum 78	Au gold 79	Hg mercury 80	Ti thalium 81
Fr francium 87	Ra radium 88	Lr lawrencium 103	Rf rutherfordium 104	Db dubnium 105	Sg seaborgium 106	Bh bohrium 107	Hs hassium 108	Mt meitnerium 109	Uun ununnilium 110	Uuu unununium 111	Uub ununbium 112	

| La lanthanum 57 | Ce cerium 58 | Pr praseodymium 59 | Nd neodymium 60 | Pm promethium 61 | Sm samarium 62 | Eu europium 63 | Gd gadolinium 64 | Tb terbium 65 | Dy dysprosium 66 | Ho holmium 67 |
| Ac actinium 89 | Th thorium 90 | Pa protactinium 91 | U uranium 92 | Np neptunium 93 | Pu plutonium 94 | Am americium 95 | Cm curium 96 | Bk berkelium 97 | Cf californium 98 | Es einsteinium 99 |

HOW DOES A PERIODIC TABLE WORK?

The periodic table is a list of all the elements, arranged in such a way that elements with similar properties are grouped together. Each element in the table is given a number, called an *atomic number*. This indicates the number of protons the atom has. A single atom has the same number of protons as electrons. Elements with the same number of electrons in their outer shells are grouped together in the table.

The groups are hydrogen, alkali and alkali earth metals, main metals, transition, and other metals, nonmetals and semi-metals, noble gas nonmetals, and the lanthanide and the actinide series.

				He helium 2
C carbon 6	N nitrogen 7	O oxygen 8	F fluorine 9	Ne neon 10
Si silicon 14	P phosphorus 15	S sulphur 16	Cl chlorine 17	Ar argon 18
Ge germanium 32	As arsenic 33	Se selenium 34	Br bromine 35	Kr krypton 36
Sn tin 50	Sb antimony 51	Te tellurium 52	I iodine 53	Xe xenon 54
Pb lead 82	Bi bismuth 83	Po polonium 84	At astatine 85	Rn radon 86

Er erbium 68	Tm thulium 69	Yb ytterbium 70
Fm fermium 100	Md mendelevium 101	No nobelium 102

FACT FILE

Many pure elements occur in different forms. Carbon can be a black powder like soot, or crystals like the hard gray graphite used in pencil leads or the glassy crystals of diamonds. Organic compounds always contain the element carbon.

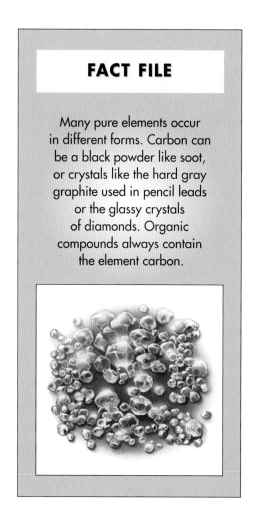

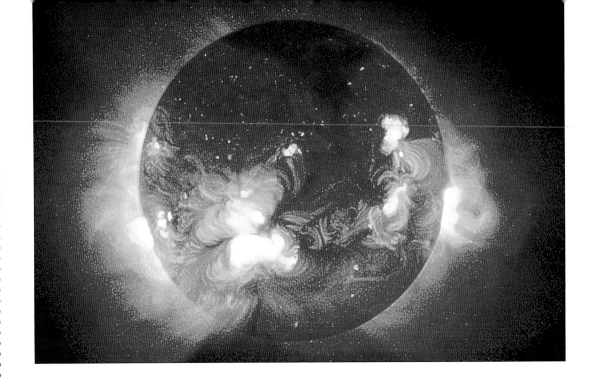

HOW DOES LIGHT TRAVEL?

Light is a form of electromagnetic radiation. It travels as waves that pass freely through space, even in the absence of air. Light waves have a wavelength, and light is the visible part of these waves.

Nearly all of the light and energy reaching the earth comes from the sun, which is powered by a continuous thermonuclear reaction like a gigantic hydrogen bomb.

Although light travels only in straight lines, it can be made to bend around curves and angles using optical fibers. These are bundles of very thin strands of exceptionally clear glass. The fibers are treated so that their outer surfaces reflect light. When light is shone in one end of the bundle, it passes along the fibers, reflecting from the sides as they curve. Eventually light emerges at the far end.

FACT FILE

As light is split by water droplets into a rainbow, the colors produced are always in the same sequence: red, orange, yellow, green, blue, indigo, and violet.

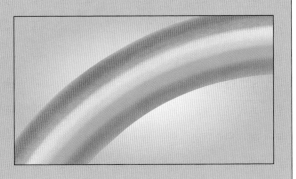

WHERE IS RUST FOUND?

Rust is the reddish-brown matter that gathers on the surface of certain metals when they are exposed to moisture. The term *rust* usually means iron rust, which is made up of hydrated iron oxide. Rust develops in a process called *oxidation*, which is the mixing of oxygen with iron.

Rust not only corrodes the surface, it also weakens the metal. If sheets of iron acquire rust holes, nails will rust off after a lengthy exposure to air and moisture. Iron can be mixed with various chemicals to create rust-resistant metals called *stainless steel*. If a metal like iron or steel is not rust-resistant, the action of oxygen can be combatted by keeping it dry or coating it with a resistant covering, like paint or chrome. Similarly, we can protect polished metals by wiping them with a cloth soaked in oil. Other ways of preventing rust include wrapping metals in chemically treated paper or coating them with grease or spray-on plastics.

FACT FILE

You would not want to eat with rusty silverware, so chromium is added to the steel to make an alloy called *stainless steel*. Unlike other metals, stainless steel will not react with acids in foods.

WHERE IS NASA LOCATED?

The National Aeronautics and Space Administration (NASA) is located on Merritt Island, across from Cape Canaveral. People often say it is located at Cape Canaveral because it was formerly located there.

NASA tests, repairs, and launches space shuttles at Kennedy Space Center. To prepare a shuttle for launch, workers in the 52-story vehicle assembly building attach the external fuel tank to the orbiter (the craft that carries the crew) and two booster rockets.

A large tractor-like machine called a *crawler* then carries the shuttle to one of two launch pads.

FACT FILE

With the help of robots and special equipment, astronauts are able to carry out difficult repairs on satellites and space stations.

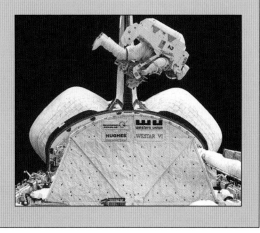

WHEN WAS YEAST FIRST USED IN BAKING?

The ancient Egyptians were the first people to produce a yeast-raised bread after discovering that it was the yeast which made bread rise.

Yeast is actually a one-celled plant so small it can be seen only under a microscope. As they grow and reproduce, substances called *enzymes*, invertase and zymase, are produced. It is these enzymes which trigger the process of fermentation, by which starch is changed to sugar and then sugar is changed to alcohol, carbon dioxide, and energy.

FACT FILE

The first bread was made in Neolithic times, nearly 12,000 years ago. It was probably made from coarsely crushed grain mixed with water. The resulting dough was probably laid on heated stones and baked by covering it with hot ashes.

Making bread rise is one of the many ways in which we can use the carbon dioxide gas formed in this way.

When making bread today, breadmakers add sugar and yeast to the dough. The starch and sugar in the dough acts as food for the yeast. When carbon dioxide is produced, it forms bubbles inside the loaf and the heat of the oven causes the gas to expand. This process makes the bread rise even more. When the carbon dioxide is dispersed by the heat, a light, dry loaf results.

WHERE WOULD SOOT BE HARMFUL?

Soot is a black or dark-brown substance found in smoke, which is particularly harmful to the lungs and the respiratory system. It is made up mostly of tiny particles of carbon, which have a diameter less than $^1/_{50}$ the width of a human hair. These particles are created when fuels such as coal, wood, or oil, all of which contain carbon, do not burn completely. Soot is one of the major forms of air pollution. It sticks to any surface it touches. It also causes enormous damage to property. In many cities, soot has left buildings looking dingy and dirty. Soot can eventually damage the surfaces of buildings by reacting chemically with them.

FACT FILE

Although soot is a pollutant, it can be useful as a pigment. Two kinds of soot used as pigments are bister and lampblack.

WHERE WOULD YOU FIND CARBON?

Carbon is found in all living things. It is one of the most familiar and important chemical elements. Yet, carbon makes up only 0.032 percent of the earth's crust. Carbon is the main component of such fuels as coal, petroleum, and natural gas. Carbon is also found in most plastics, many of which are derived from carbon fuels. Carbon has the chemical symbol C. Pure carbon occurs in four forms: (1) diamond, (2) graphite (as used in pencils), (3) amorphous carbons, and (4) fullerenes. The four forms have different crystalline structures. This means that their atoms are arranged differently. The various forms of carbon differ greatly in hardness and other properties, depending on how their atoms are arranged.

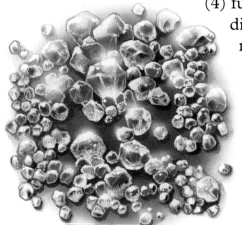

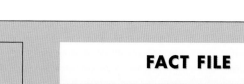

FACT FILE

Diamond is the hardest naturally occurring substance known and one of the most valuable. Natural diamonds form in the rock beneath the earth's crust, where high temperature and pressure cause carbon atoms to make strong bonds with other carbon atoms and to crystallize.

WHERE DOES THE WORD
RADAR COME FROM?

The word *radar* comes from radio detection and ranging. Radar is a scientific method used to detect and locate moving or fixed objects. Radar can determine the direction, distance, height, and speed of objects that are much too far away for the human eye to see. It can find objects as small as insects or as large as mountains. Radar can even operate effectively at night and in heavy fog, rain, or snow.

Almost every radar set works by sending radio waves towards an object and receiving the waves reflected from that object. The time it takes for the reflected waves to return indicates the object's range, that is, how far away it is. The direction from which the reflected waves return tells us the object's location.

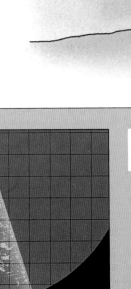

FACT FILE

Radar uses microwave radiation to detect distant objects. The microwaves usually scan around in a circle, and the echoes sent back produce an image on a screen.

WHAT ARE GEARS?

A gear is a mechanical device that transfers rotating motion and power from one part of a machine to another. Gears are produced in a wide range of sizes and vary greatly in use. They range from the tiny gears that drive the hands of a watch to the huge gears that turn the propeller of a tanker. A simple gear consists of a metal wheel or disk with slots called *teeth* around the edge. Gears always work in pairs. The teeth of one gear mesh with the teeth of the other. Each gear has a metal axle in the middle. The axle of one gear is connected to a power source, such as an electric motor. When the power axle turns, its gear turns and causes the second gear to rotate in the opposite direction. This action powers the axle of the second gear to do useful work.

FACT FILE

A bicycle's gear system makes pedaling easier at certain times. Low gears, which make it easy to pedal up hills or against the wind, rotate the rear wheel only a little during each turn of the pedals.

WHERE DOES NITRIC ACID OCCUR NATURALLY?

Nitric acid was one of the first acids known and was used in experiments by alchemists and other scientists beginning with the Middle Ages.

Nitric acid is produced naturally in large quantities during thunderstorms, and falls to the ground in rain. Rain is a very weak solution of nitric acid. The production of nitric acid in thunderstorms enables the nitrogen from the air to combine with the soil in a form that can be used by plants.

As a strong inorganic acid, nitric acid has many industrial uses. One of its major uses is for the production of explosives and fertilizers.

FACT FILE

As a powerful oxidizing agent, nitric acid can actually dissolve many metals, but it does not attack gold and platinum. We can tell whether gold or platinum is genuine by applying a drop of nitric acid.

WHERE DOES HELIUM COME FROM?

Helium is a lightweight gas and chemical element which makes up a tiny fraction of the earth's matter. It is found in natural gas deposits in the atmosphere, which contains about 5 parts of helium to every million parts of air. Nevertheless, because the sun and other stars are made largely of helium and hydrogen, it is actually one of the most common elements in the universe. In fact, the basic energy of stars comes from hydrogen atoms joining together to form helium atoms.

Because it is so light, helium constantly drifts into space away from the atmosphere, and is replaced by radioactive matter that shoots out alpha particles. A common use for helium is for filling balloons, mainly for scientific research. Because helium is lighter than air, the balloons are able to rise to very high altitudes. In the air, helium has almost the same lifting ability as hydrogen, but unlike hydrogen, it will not burn, which makes safer.

FACT FILE

Deep-sea divers often breathe a mixture of helium and oxygen to avoid a painful illness which frequently occurs at depths below 100 feet (30 meters), called *nitrogen narcosis*.

WHERE IS METAMORPHIC ROCK FOUND?

Metamorphic rock is found in the earth's crust, along with igneous and sedimentary rocks. Igneous rocks are formed when melted rock deep inside the crust cools and hardens, or erupts at the surface as lava. Sedimentary rocks develop from materials that once were part of older rocks or of plants or animals. These materials were worn away from the land. Then, they are collected in low places,

FACT FILE

The earth's crust is moving all the time. Here, you can see the land has been pushed into giant folds.

layer upon layer, and hardened into rock. Many sedimentary rocks contain shells, bones, and other remains of living things. Such remains, or the impressions of such remain, in sedimentary rocks are called *fossils*. Metamorphic rocks are formed deep in the crust when igneous and sedimentary rocks are changed by heat and the weight of the crust presses on them.

WHERE IS THE MANTLE?

Beneath the earth's crust is a sphere of hot rock and metal. By studying the records of earthquake waves, scientists have learned that the inside of the earth is divided into three parts: the mantle, the outer core, and the inner core.

The mantle is a thick layer of rock below the crust. It goes down about 1,800 miles (2,900 km). The rock in the mantle is made of silicon, oxygen, aluminium, iron, and magnesium. The uppermost part of the mantle has a temperature of about 1600°F (870°C). The temperature gradually increases to about 8000°F (4400°C) in the deepest part of the mantle. The outer core begins about 1,800 miles (2,900 km) below the earth's surface. The ball-shaped inner core lies within the outer core and makes up the middle of the earth.

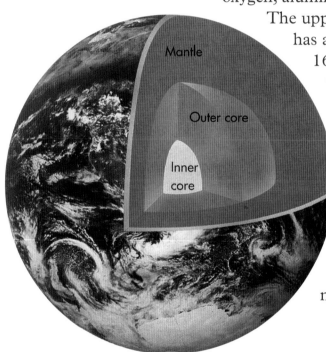

Mantle

Outer core

Inner core

FACT FILE

The inner core rotates more rapidly than the remainder of the earth. During a period of about 400 years, the inner core rotates around the earth's axis one more time than the surface does.

WHY ARE ATOMS EVERYWHERE?

Atoms are the tiny particles that make up the universe. Enormous amounts of energy are locked inside atoms. Atoms are the tiniest particles into which a substance can be divided without changing into something else. Atoms consist almost entirely of open space, in which tiny particles orbit the central particle, or nucleus. These particles travel so fast that they seem to be solid.

Atoms are so miniscule that the smallest particle visible to the naked eye would contain about one million billion atoms. Despite their tiny size, atoms can be seen individually under very powerful electron microscopes.

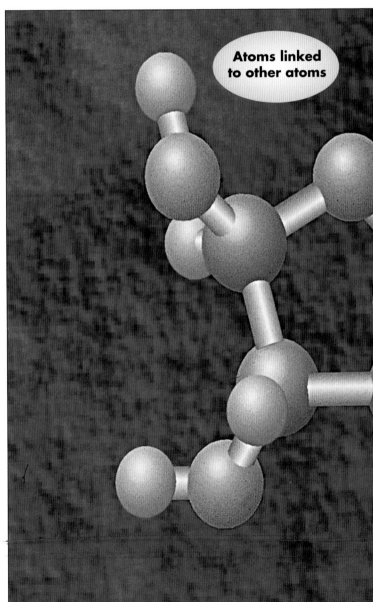

Atoms linked to other atoms

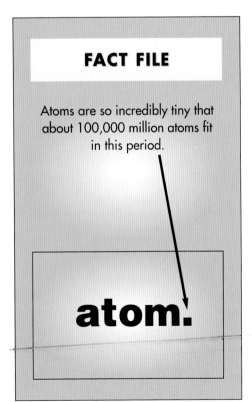

FACT FILE

Atoms are so incredibly tiny that about 100,000 million atoms fit in this period.

atom.

WHY IS QUANTUM PHYSICS USED?

Quantum physics helps us to understand how energy is used or released by atoms. Negatively charged electrons circle around the positively charged nucleus of the atom. They stay in the same orbit until it is disturbed. Each orbit has its own level of energy. If more energy is added, the electron jumps into another orbit, absorbing the extra energy. Then, when it drops back again into its original orbit, it releases this energy as heat or light. This tiny packet of energy is called a *quantum*. It is not possible to measure exactly where a subatomic particle is and how fast it is moving, because that will disturb the particle and change its characteristics.

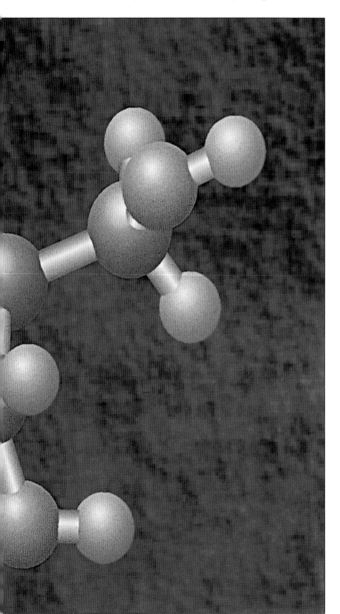

FACT FILE

An atom becomes linked to other atoms by electrical bonds, which work much like chemical hooks. Some atoms carry only one of these hooks, while others may have many. Atoms with many hooks can build up with other atoms into complicated molecules or chemical compounds.

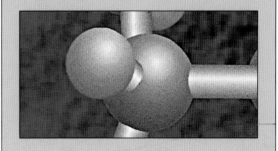

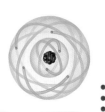

Neutral

Acid

Alkaline

WHAT IS LITMUS PAPER USED FOR?

Litmus paper is a quick way to test a liquid to see whether it is acid or alkaline.

Dyes, called *indicators*, show very quickly if a substance dissolved in water is acid or alkaline. One of these dyes is litmus. If a piece of litmus paper is dipped into a solution, it immediately turns red if the solution is acid. If the solution is alkaline, the litmus paper turns blue.

A dye similar to litmus is present in some red vegetables, such as red cabbage and beetroot. This dye changes color in the same way during cooking. If your tap water is hard, or alkaline, the vegetables will turn a deep purplish-blue.

FACT FILE

Bee stings are acidic. An acid is neutralized by an alkali, which will reduce the painful effects of a bee sting. Soap is alkaline, so it will help lessen the effect of the sting if it is rubbed on the skin.

HOW DO CRYSTALS FORM?

Crystals are formed from dissolved substances or when molten substances cool slowly. As the solutions evaporate or the melted materials cool, their atoms are forced closer together, producing a crystal. The crystal gradually grows as the process continues. Some crystals grow into complicated and beautiful shapes, which are often very brightly colored.

Crystals are solid substances that have their atoms arranged in regular patterns. Most naturally occurring substances form crystals under the right conditions, though they are not always apparent.

FACT FILE

Snowflakes are made up of millions of ice crystals. If you were to look at them under a microscope, each would appear to be a different pattern.

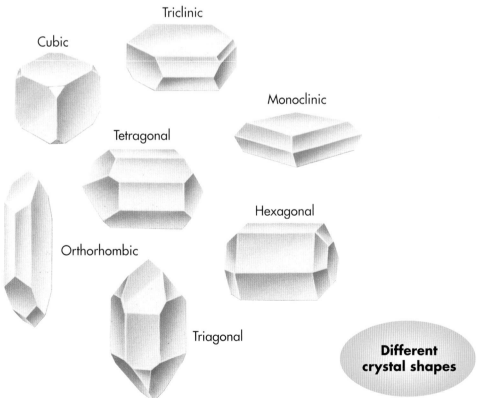

Cubic

Triclinic

Monoclinic

Tetragonal

Hexagonal

Orthorhombic

Triagonal

Different crystal shapes

HOW DOES A COMPASS WORK?

The magnetized needle on a compass aligns itself with the earth's field of magnetic force.

Electrical currents influence other electrical currents. This force is called *magnetism*. The core of the earth actually functions like a huge magnet. On a compass, the magnetized needle aligns itself towards the earth's field of magnetic force. The needle is balanced on a pointed pin and floats on oil to allow it to rotate freely without friction.

A compass must be used carefully. If it is near any object that can distort the earth's magnetic field, it will give a false reading. A nearby object made of iron or steel will cause the compass needle to swing wildly.

FACT FILE

Many animals, such as this albatross, are able to travel great distances in order to arrive at a particular destination. They are able to find their way accurately because of tiny magnetic particles found in their organs. These act in the same manner as a compass.

How is an Electromagnet Made?

FACT FILE

One of the most important uses of magnets is in electric motors, which power machines ranging from small toys to enormous railway engines. Video and audio tapes also depend on magnetism.

Electromagnets can produce magnetism only when an electrical current passes through them. They usually consist of a metal core made of iron or similar material, around which are wrapped many coils of thin, insulated wire. The metal core becomes magnetized when an electric current passes through the wire coil, but the effect disappears immediately when the current is shut off. Very powerful electromagnets can be made by using many coils and strong electrical currents.

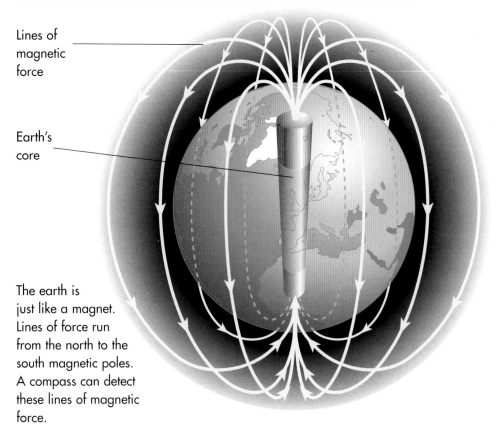

Lines of magnetic force

Earth's core

The earth is just like a magnet. Lines of force run from the north to the south magnetic poles. A compass can detect these lines of magnetic force.